T0000520

LITERATURE FOR A CHANGING PLANET

THE OXFORD RESEARCH CENTRE IN THE
HUMANITIES / PRINCETON UNIVERSITY PRESS
LECTURES IN EUROPEAN CULTURE

LITERATURE
for a
CHANGING
PLANET

MARTIN
PUCHNER

PRINCETON UNIVERSITY PRESS
Princeton & Oxford

Copyright © 2022 by Princeton University Press

Princeton University Press is committed to the protection of copyright and the intellectual property our authors entrust to us. Copyright promotes the progress and integrity of knowledge. Thank you for supporting free speech and the global exchange of ideas by purchasing an authorized edition of this book. If you wish to reproduce or distribute any part of it in any form, please obtain permission.

Requests for permission to reproduce material from this work should be sent to permissions@press.princeton.edu

Published by Princeton University Press
41 William Street, Princeton, New Jersey 08540
6 Oxford Street, Woodstock, Oxfordshire OX20 1TR

press.princeton.edu

All Rights Reserved

Library of Congress Cataloging-in-Publication Data

Names: Puchner, Martin, 1969– author.
Title: Literature for a changing planet / Martin Puchner.
Description: Princeton : Princeton University Press, 2022. |
    Includes bibliographical references and index.
Identifiers: LCCN 2021016499 (print) | LCCN 2021016500 (ebook) |
    ISBN 9780691213750 (hardback) | ISBN 9780691230429 (ebook)
Subjects: LCSH: Ecocriticism. | Literature—History and criticism. |
    Climatic changes in literature. | BISAC: LITERARY CRITICISM/
    Comparative Literature | LITERARY CRITICISM/General |
    LCGFT: Literary criticism.
Classification: LCC PN98.E36 P86 2022 (print) | LCC PN98.E36 (ebook) |
    DDC 809/.9336—dc23
LC record available at https://lccn.loc.gov/2021016499
LC ebook record available at https://lccn.loc.gov/2021016500

British Library Cataloging-in-Publication Data is available

Editorial: Ben Tate and Josh Drake
Production Editorial: Ellen Foos
Text Design: Chris Ferrante
Jacket art and design by Nuno Moreira
Production: Danielle Amatucci
Publicity: Jodi Price and Carmen Jimenez
Copyeditor: Daniel Simon

This book has been composed in Adobe Caslon and Big Caslon

Printed on acid-free paper. ∞

Printed in the United States of America

10 9 8 7 6 5 4 3 2 1

FOR USCHI AND DAVID

CONTENTS

LITERATURE FOR A CHANGING PLANET

LITERATURE FOR A CHANGING PLANET

ONE HUNDRED AND SIXTY million years ago, in the inner region of the asteroid belt, a piece of rock was separated from its companions by the subtle interplay of gravitational forces. Slowly, it drifted away, a tiny object about thirty miles across, calmly following its new trajectory through the expanse of space. After three hundred million miles of undisturbed travel at the steady speed of forty thousand miles per hour, the rock suddenly encountered resistance when an atmospheric cloud slowed its progress, transforming momentum into heat. A moment later, the rock hit water and land. In less than a second, it burrowed some twelve miles into the continental crust, before coming to a complete halt.[1]

Around it, mayhem ensued. The forces unleashed by the impact were hundreds of billions of times as large as the two atomic bombs that would devastate Hiroshima and Nagasaki. The stray asteroid hit earth near the Yucatan Peninsula in southern Mexico, where sixty-six million years later the Spaniard Hernán Cortés would land with his group of adventurers, equipped with steel, horses, and germs, destroying an entire culture. The asteroid did its work of destruction through the sheer force of impact, unleashing a tsunami that reached all the way to Florida and Texas. Large amounts of debris were thrown up into the atmosphere, where they became burning projectiles that rained back down onto earth, turning everything within their reach into an inferno. Shockwaves led to a cascade of earthquakes and volcanic eruptions across the globe.

The long-term impact was even more devastating. Acid rains and a spike in CO_2 levels led to a greenhouse effect. Worse still was the dust cloud that blocked the sun, sharply reducing photosynthesis, which interrupted the entire food chain. The bigger the animals, the higher up in the food chain, the worse off they were. When several years later plants started to grow again from seeds and roots, many of the larger animal species had already died out, all land-based dinosaurs among them.

Over the next sixty-six million years, the gravely disturbed ecosystem of planet earth adjusted. All it needed was time, time for photosynthesis to start again, time for random mutations to produce better adaptations for particular niches and for old species to move to different habitats. Life resumed but on a smaller scale than before, favoring bacteria and mammals, which multiplied thanks to the absence of large predators. What remained of the dinosaurs took to the air, picking off small mammals from time to time in memory of their former supremacy. Over time, the trauma of the collision was almost forgotten, and even the crater, sixty-two miles wide and nineteen miles deep, filled in. It was almost as if the stray meteorite had never hit home.

Today, it's not a disturbance in the solar system that is causing a mass extinction, nor a projectile hailing from a hundred and sixty million years ago and three hundred million miles away. This time around, the disturbance is entirely homegrown: an unfeathered biped stalking the dinosaur-free surface of the earth. It doesn't look like much, this scraggly creature, but it has a few neat tricks up its sleeve. For one thing, it can sweat, which means that it can outrun any land-based life-form—even gazelles, panthers, and horses—over long distances, anything that gets hot and pants, while this two-legged runner sweats and therefore cools in the wind. Also, it's not particular in its choice of foods, eating pretty much anything, from roots, leaves, and fruits to worms, insects, and other mammals; in a pinch, it even eats its own.[2]

This omnivore emerged less than a million years ago, took on modern form some eight hundred thousand years later, and soon learned to use all kinds of tools, thanks to fine motor skills and opposable thumbs.

Even more important were its vocal cords, which allowed for a wide range of sounds that formed the basis for a sophisticated sound-based language, which enabled coordination on an unprecedented scale. Moving in hordes, held together by ever better forms of communication, this species fanned out across the surface of the earth, hunting and gathering everything it its path. It also liked to play with fire, not on the scale of the asteroid, but with small fires that allowed it to eat even more things, filling its weak stomach with hard roots, stems, berries, and cooked meats. Soon, it would use fire to burn down steppes to drive other animals into its traps or to create new pastures for its herds. Slowly, this vocalizing arsonist was remaking the earth to suit its needs.

The makeover of earth gained speed ten thousand years ago, when the creature got tired of running. It had figured out how to grow plants that yielded more calories and how to domesticate animals, and it was so pleased with these inventions that it decided to settle down. This was not the healthiest of lifestyles because crops could fail, and domesticated animals led to new diseases, viruses and plagues that sprung from animals to humans and decimated the settled population with predictable frequency. But the new mode of life also had advantages: intensive agriculture and cities allowed for a new division of labor, leading to new inventions such as writing, which supercharged the use of language, one of the creature's most valuable tools. Cities spread, populations increased, and the new settled life was changing the earth again, as forests were chopped down to build houses and to generate heat.

Things were going really well for this retired long-distance runner as it accumulated the knowledge to manipulate the world ever more effectively. By the year zero, it reached one hundred and ninety million; in 1700, six hundred million. Things sped up with industrialization, thanks to energy harnessed from animals, flowing water, and increasingly from things that could be scratched from below the surface of the earth, such as coal and oil. With so much energy at its disposal, the creature needed to sweat less and less, and reproduced more and more: nine hundred and ninety million in 1900; two billion in 1928; three billion in 1960; four billion in 1975; five billion in 1987; and six billion in 1999. In terms of biomass, it was still dwarfed by earthworms and bacteria (some of them living inside its intestines), but in all other respects, it had remade the earth in its own image.

It had also made a mess of it: sedentary life, intensive agriculture, population explosion, and carbon extraction were leading to another massive species extinction caused by land-loss, pesticides, and rising CO_2 levels that began to fry the planet. As the population nears eight billion, there can no longer be any doubt that something terrible is happening: this information-hoarding settler is wreaking havoc on a meteoritic scale.

How to tell the story of humans as meteorite? The scale is beyond human imagining because of the magnitudes involved, but also because of time. A population explosion taking ten thousand years sounds very different from a projectile hitting earth at forty thousand miles an hour, but in evolutionary terms, the two are pretty much the same: they happen too fast for evolution to adjust. The problem is not change itself, for species change and go extinct all the time. The climate, too, is in constant flux, responding to forces both homegrown and hailing from the outer reaches of the solar system. If there is a lesson to be learned from the meteorite, it's that earth exists in a galactic environment from which it can never isolate itself completely.

The problem is not change, but the rate of change: sudden, in evolutionary terms, is anything that's faster than what random mutations can adapt to over hundreds of thousands of years. Yet humans learned how to outpace evolution by passing down information through language and other storage systems, transmitting from generation to generation an increasing store of knowledge; and when writing came along, it became possible to preserve, spread, and increase information within a few generations. This form of information management jump-starts a process infinitely faster than evolution; information is the fuel that accelerates human development into something breathtakingly fast—as fast as a meteorite.

If one problem of representation is speed, the other is effect. Even though evolution is constantly changing, it produces finely calibrated ecosystems that are breathtaking in their complexity and fragility at any given time. Humans are smashing this system to pieces, creating ripple effects every bit as devastating as the earthquakes and volcanic eruptions caused by the meteorite. But capturing complexity—including feedback loops, tipping points, cascades of cause and effect that keep branching off—is difficult, and we haven't yet learned how to do it effectively.

Then, also, there is the question of agency. If we are to tell the story of humans as a meteorite, we are telling a collective history of us all. But aren't some more involved than others? The ones who used fire; the ones who invented language; the ones who stopped running and decided to settle down; the ones who switched to intensive agriculture; the ones who came up with writing and other storage media; the ones who extracted oil and coal; the ones who indulged in excessive consumption. If *we* are the meteorite, it is also true that some of us are more directly responsible than others by contributing more to the process that separated us from the rest of evolution and put us on a collision course with ourselves.

The challenges of scale, complexity, and agency are problems of narrative. Stories require that we construct a world, the setting into which we place an agent who undertakes an action. But what kinds of stories should these be? Morality tales that assign blame, creating villains? Cautionary tales that pinpoint a wrong turn taken long ago? Stories of unintended consequences and devastating effects? Dire warnings that we are in the middle of an inferno without quite realizing it, blinded by our short lives and even shorter attention spans?

Stories matter terribly to humans because whenever these born runners slow down for just a moment, they begin to tell one another stories, stories that capture experiences that need to be passed down, stories that create cohesion and cooperation within groups, stories that articulate shared values by explaining significant events in the past. Humans are born storytellers; they want to know where they come from and who is to blame for their difficulties.

Stories are powerful motivators, and they can be terribly misleading. There is competition among stories, a competition for attention (which stories do we listen to?), for authority (which stories do we believe in?), and for survival (which stories get passed down to the next generation?), which is why it matters what kinds of stories get told and how existing ones are interpreted.

Climate scientists have woken up to the power of stories. For the past forty years, their strategy had been to do better climate science, assuming that improved models and more accurate predictions would translate into appropriate changes in policy and behavior. The strategy hasn't worked, and now scientists are asking for stories that pinpoint agency, that capture complexity, that make ten thousand years seem like a millisecond collision. What is needed are new stories as well as new ways of understanding old ones. The power of stories—seductive, misleading, and potentially transformative—needs to be harnessed to a new purpose: mitigating climate change.[3]

The good news is that there is an entire discipline devoted to storytelling: literary studies. In particular, there has emerged over the past several decades a thriving subdiscipline of ecocriticism that has paid attention to everything from nature writing inspired by Henry Thoreau's *Walden*, of 1854, to Rachel Carson's *Silent Spring*, of 1962, with its powerful focus on pollution.[4] More recently, the field has expanded to study the literary representations of the industrial revolution, the age of oil, and of colonialism, with additional attention to climate justice in the United States and elsewhere.[5]

Unfortunately, the insights of ecocriticism have not been as widely noted outside the field as they should be. This is in part because literary studies have suffered a loss in recognition and authority, along with many other humanities disciplines, as expressed in plummeting enrollment numbers and declining jobs. Yet climate change is also sidelined within literary studies.

MFA programs, important generators of stories in the United States, have traditionally been concerned more with style and voice than ideas and science, and few have included teachers who pay sustained attention to the environment.[6] The same is true in the discipline of world literature, in which few scholars, until quite recently, have paid attention to the environment.[7]

All this is changing now as a gathering sense of crisis is putting all disciplines and areas of knowledge on alert. This book is part of a movement to bring the broader field of literature and storytelling to the looming crisis of climate change. In the process, I will make an argument in favor of large timescales as particularly important for understanding the relation between storytelling and the environment. While environmental degradation and rising CO_2 levels have steeply accelerated in the last two hundred years, the decisions and habits that set humans on the course toward climate disaster go much further back, making it crucial to study the distant past of storytelling.[8] Such larger time spans are available through the concept of world literature and its commitment to understanding literature as a single, interrelated system, which is why the history of world literature will play an important role in these pages. Additionally, I believe that the deep history of world literature can offer writers and storytellers a much broader set of models upon which to draw when it comes to telling new stories about humans and their planet. By bringing together insights from ecocriticism, world literature, and narrative studies, this book hopes to enhance the role of literature in the conversation about climate change, a conversation too important to take place without the humanities.[9]

CHAPTER ONE

READING IN A WARMING WORLD

HOW SHOULD WE HUMANS narrate our self-made climate disaster? In a sense, we have been doing it all along. All great works of literature concern themselves with a world reshaped by human hands and are therefore potential sources for understanding the process by which humans have changed their environment. The only challenge is to learn how to read these works with a sustained attention to climate change. They don't always yield to this kind of reading easily because they were not made for this purpose. Sometimes, they hide or sideline the traces of human-made climate change by defending the way of life that caused that change and by being unaware of climate change itself. Yet works of world literature can be made to yield their significance if we ask the right questions, focus on the right details, and embed those details in the larger societal processes that put us on our current, disastrous path.

To exemplify the kind of reading I have in mind, one inspired by ecocriticism, I want to begin with a source text of literature, arguably the first great work of world literature: the *Epic of Gilgamesh*. Its earliest form dates back more than four thousand years, but the work took on canonical form seven hundred years later, when it came to dominate an entire region for over a millennium. But then, some time before the Common Era, it disappeared, along with the cuneiform writing system in which it was written. By chance, the text was unearthed again two thousand years later, in the 1840s, by the restless adventurer Austen Henry Layard while he was digging for Nineveh, the biblical city once located on the Euphrates River.[1] Through luck and perseverance—and the reading of the Hebrew Bible—Layard hit upon the burnt-down library of Ashurbanipal, an Assyrian king who had collected the clay tablets that contained this ancient epic. (When Ashurbanipal's library went up in flames, the clay tablets had hardened, inadvertently preserving this masterpiece for millennia underground.)

Finding the epic was one thing; reading it, another. It took another couple of decades to decode the forgotten cuneiform script, a feat that was achieved at the British Library, whither Layard had transported the tablets.[2] The deciphering of this text was headline news because this oldest surviving masterpiece contained shocking information for Victorian England: a text older than the Old Testament included an identical story of Noah and the Flood. What were Christian believers to make of this remarkable coincidence? What were the implications for the status of the Old Testament as holy scripture?

Today, the provocative potential of the story of the flood is undiminished, though for different reasons: I regard it as a key text when it comes to climate change.[3]

Despite the striking similarities, the two flood stories, in the *Epic of Gilgamesh* and in the Hebrew Bible, are also quite different. In the Hebrew Bible, we read:

> And the Lord saw that the evil of the human creature was great on the earth and that every scheme of his heart's devising was only perpetually evil. And the Lord regretted having made the human on earth and was grieved to the heart. And the Lord said, "I will wipe out the human race I created from the face of the earth, from human to cattle to crawling thing to the fowl of the heavens, for I regret that I have made them."[4]

As translated by Robert Alter, the flood is clearly presented as punishment: humans have been violating God's commands, leading God to regret that he ever made them. He comes to view the creation of humans as a mistake that has to be undone. The mistake encompasses not just humans; all living creatures are apparently guilty by association and must be wiped out as well. It is only thanks to Noah, the one good man, that humans, along with all the other animals, survive.

In the *Epic of Gilgamesh*, the details of survival are similar: the Noah-like Utnapishtim builds a large boat, saves his family as well as the family of animals, sends out birds to see whether the waters are receding, and rejoices when one of them returns with a twig in its beak—these were the details so strikingly similar to the Bible that disturbed Victorian England.

Yet even if the details are similar, the moral of the story is different. In the *Epic of Gilgamesh*, the flood is not part of the main story but merely an interpolated tale told by Utnapishtim to Gilgamesh toward the end of the epic. Instead of framing the story as one of divine retribution, Utnapishtim begins his tale simply by saying that the gods had resolved to send a deluge, giving no reason as to why they had done so. One of the gods reveals the gods' secret plan of destruction and instructs Utnapishtim to build a boat and safeguard samples of the world's fauna. When the ordeal is over, a goddess accuses the great god Enlil of having brought on the deluge "irrationally."[5] To be sure, she concedes, in a purely hypothetical manner: "punish the wrongdoer for his wrongdoing, / and punish the transgressor for his transgressions / But be lenient."[6] However, she then suggests less extreme measures that would have been more appropriate: "Let the lion rise up to diminish the human race"; "Let the wolf rise up to diminish the human race"; "let famine rise up to wreak havoc in the land"; "let pestilence rise up to wreak havoc in the land."[7] The point here is not sin and punishment, but something closer to population control. The human race has grown too populous and needs to be culled. There are better ways of doing so than by destroying everything through a flood, the goddess is saying, and the epic confirms her point of view.

Despite the fact that we have now, once again, this second, earlier version of the Flood at our disposal, the biblical version continues to dominate. One reason may be that the debate about climate change tends to be charged morally with ideas of sin and punishment, transgression and retribution; another is, of course, that the Hebrew Bible is more influential than the *Epic of Gilgamesh*. Or are these the same reason? Biblical morality is shaping current thinking about the climate more than it should. True, one might argue that seeing climate change through a moral lens makes sense to the extent that human-made climate change is our fault. Perhaps we must even follow Noah and save ourselves by building a new ark (is this what Elon Musk is doing with his mission to Mars?). The question of agency and responsibility is everywhere, and the Old Testament seems to offer a powerful warning in the form of a morality tale as well as a solution.

Today, however, it is becoming clear that the religious fable of righteousness and sin is not effective in pinpointing cause and effect for human-induced climate change, nor in mitigating it. The righteous recycler who unplugs from the grid and lives a virtuous zero-emissions life will not save humans. If a story of the Flood is useful at all—and it may be better to jettison it entirely—the one from the *Epic of Gilgamesh*, less concerned with sin and punishment, and more with population control and the relation between humans and their environment, is probably better.

Mesopotamians, unlike inhabitants of arid Jerusalem, where the idea of a flood must have come as a surprise, experienced floods on a regular basis. Living between two large rivers, the Tigris and the Euphrates, they had been able to invent intensive agriculture because of the regular flooding that brought new soil and nutrients to their fields (the word *Mesopotamia*, in Greek, means "land between the rivers"). The problem was how to control these periodic floods. For this purpose, Mesopotamians created an elaborate system of canals, something that is also mentioned in the *Epic of Gilgamesh*. It was the first attempt to control the environment by means of a large engineering project. The canals worked astonishingly well, until they didn't, leading to inevitable flooding, which reminded humans, or should have reminded humans, that environmental engineering, then as now, had its limits and its risks. As more people settled in the fertile floodplains, more people were exposed to violent floods, beginning a high-stakes cycle that has continued to this day. Among many other things, the *Epic of Gilgamesh* is a warning against this form of hubris.

While the flood got all the original headlines, there are other, more trenchant parts of the *Epic of Gilgamesh* that speak to how settled humans construct their relationship to the environment. The epic begins with a crisis: a wild creature has been interfering with the natural order of things. It has destroyed human traps; it has filled in pits that are meant to catch wildlife; it has helped other animals escape from humans. One hunter has spotted the creature: it has fur all over its body, including a long mane on its head; it feeds on grass alongside gazelles and joins other animals at the watering hole.

The epic's account of this wild creature is at least as significant, from an environmental perspective, as the flood. For this creature is actually some sort of a human, named Enkidu. We know this because he has been created by the gods specifically to rein in Gilgamesh, king of Uruk, who doesn't know what to do with his strength. Gilgamesh creates chaos by doing whatever he wants, which is mostly doing battle with men and raping women. Something has to change, so the gods have taken clay and molded Enkidu out of it. But for the time being, Enkidu lives with the animals and shuns human company. He is not quite human yet.

And so, the drama of how Enkidu can be brought into human society begins. He has to shave off his beard; he has to start wearing clothes; he has to start eating cooked foods; and he has to shun the company of other animals. This is accomplished by sending out a woman who seduces him. After the seduction, the other animals reject Enkidu, and he has no choice but to throw in his lot with humans. Once he is in human society, he befriends Gilgamesh (well, first they fight, then they make up) and learns how to eat bread and drink beer. Only then has Enkidu become fully human, and the epic can turn its attention to other topics, essentially becoming an adventure story of two friends going out into the world. It's possible that they even become lovers.

What the *Epic of Gilgamesh* does here is draw a line between humans and nonhumans. Even if you are biologically a human being, you are not human as long as you live in the wilderness, as long as you graze, as long as you don't reject the wilderness and settle down, as long as you don't eat and drink the products of intensive agriculture, such as bread and beer, that have made settled life possible.

More specifically, what the epic draws between humans and humanlike wildlings isn't a line: it's a wall. Gilgamesh is famous for having rebuilt the wall around Uruk, the city over which he rules. The wall and the physical plant of the city are also what the *Epic of Gilgamesh* is visibly proud of. Before the main action begins, the *Epic* gives its readers a tour of the city:

He [Gilgamesh] built the walls of ramparted Uruk,
The lustrous treasury of hallowed Eanna!
See its upper wall, whose facing gleams like copper,
Gaze at the lower course, which nothing will equal,
Mount the stone stairway, there from days of old,
Approach Eanna, the dwelling of Ishtar,
Which no future king, no human being will equal.
Go up, pace out the walls of Uruk,
Study the foundation terrace and examine the
   brickwork.
Is not its masonry of kiln-fired brick?
And did not seven masters lay its foundations?
One square mile of city, one square mile of gardens,
One square mile of clay pits, a half square mile of
   Ishtar's dwelling,
Three and a half square miles is the measure of
   Uruk![8]

The passage reads like the script of an excited tour guide telling us where to look, explaining all the sights, praising what we see. It is a miracle, we are to understand, this ramparted city, a miracle made of clay. Clay is the material from which this city wall is made, kiln-fired bricks, and clay bricks are what the houses and temples are made of as well. Clay is such an important building material that the tour guide even mentions the clay pits from which this material is harvested.

This city, ramparted by clay bricks, is the world into which Enkidu has to be brought. It is here where wheat, harvested by clay sickles or flint, baked in clay pots, and stored in clay containers, is consumed, and where beer, stored in clay vessels, is brewed from barley. The wall that separates humans from animals separates the city from the country. The *Epic of Gilgamesh* is a text that celebrates urban living and dismisses the wilderness as unfit for human habitation.

There are lots of reasons to celebrate Uruk. The city was one of the first large urban centers in the world, concentrating as many as fifty thousand inhabitants into one small space. But to my ears, the celebration of urbanism undertaken in the epic also has a tinge of defensiveness about it—a tour guide's exaggeration. One recent scholar has suggested that Gilgamesh's impressive city wall was built as much to keep the good people of Uruk in as to keep wildlings such as Enkidu out.[9] It is true that sedentary life reduced the diversity of foods, exposed inhabitants to droughts and floods, and led to the spread of diseases. There is evidence that in the early days of agriculture, humans sometimes returned to hunting and gathering or to following their herds because of the significant drawbacks of agricultural life. Also, cities had to be defended against nomads whose diet was more diverse and who tended to be stronger. So perhaps there is an element of propaganda in the epic's praise of city living. Enkidu, after all, didn't come voluntarily. He had to be seduced into the city through cunning.[10]

As soon as the seduction of Enkidu, which is really an induction into urban living, is complete, the two friends leave the city again. Their goal is to kill the monstrous Humbaba, who lives far away, in a forest of cedars, which he guards jealously. This is the central episode in the entire epic and one in which the close friendship between Gilgamesh and Enkidu is sealed. Along the way, Gilgamesh is plagued by dreams that seem to foretell disaster, but each time Enkidu puts a more positive spin on them, convincing his friend to go on. Enkidu's past as a wildling is not entirely forgotten. On their trek through the countryside, Gilgamesh remembers that his friend used to live here, that the wilderness is where he originated. Perhaps this is what gives Enkidu the authority to interpret Gilgamesh's dreams.

Finally, after all obstacles, such as Gilgamesh's ominous dreams, have been cleared away, the much-anticipated encounter of the two friends with the monster can take place. Unsurprisingly, the great Gilgamesh vanquishes Humbaba in battle, which is described in some detail. Once more, the wilderness loses against the ruler of urban life. Intriguingly, Humbaba seems to recognize Enkidu as a fellow wildling, which is why he pleads with him for his life. "You know the lore of my forest, / And you understand all I have to say," Humbaba says to him, quite correctly.[11] But Humbaba doesn't recognize that Enkidu now denies his past and has fully sided with the city, even more so than

Gilgamesh. He eggs on Gilgamesh and convinces him to kill the monster with the zeal of a recent convert.

Their dirty work complete, the two friends begin what they have actually come to do: to fell trees. "Gilgamesh cut down the trees, / Enkidu chose the timbers," the narrators says, and Enkidu elaborates the reason.[12] Speaking to Gilgamesh, he says: "You killed the guardian by your strength, / Who else could cut through this forest of trees? / My friend, we have felled the lofty cedar, / Whose crown once pierced the sky. / I will make a door six times twelve cubits high, two times twelve cubits wide, / One cubit shall be its thickness / Its hinge pole, ferrule, and pivot box shall be unique."[13] The mythical venture to the forest and the battle with Humbaba are in fact nothing but an elaborate logging expedition, extracting a resource that is crucial for building cities.

While Uruk, the gigantic city, is mostly made from clay, its doors and roofs are made from timber. And also it is not only Uruk. More and more cities have sprung up in Mesopotamia—sedentary life isn't that bad after all—which means that there have been more and more logging expeditions leading to increased deforestation. Rulers have to bring timber from farther and farther away to feed the first urban construction boom in history. This is why the two friends have to go all the way to Lebanon, which is where Humbaba and his cedar forest are located, some seven hundred miles from Uruk. The sedentary lifestyle is remaking the landscape and requires more and more resource extraction. It is a bitter irony: the former wildling Enkidu is now working for city dwellers, destroying the environment that once sustained him. Humbaba's is not just a regular forest: it is a sacred grove, which means that it is untouched by human hands. One might translate this into the language of botany and say that it is virgin forest, the most important, environmentally, by far. Humbaba is right: Enkidu knows all about the forest and should know better, but he no longer cares. He likes his clothes, his bread, and his beer, he likes women, and above all he likes Gilgamesh, his best friend and builder of city walls.

The episode confirms the line, or wall, drawn around humanity: those who dwell in the forest are monsters and have to be killed. The forest is not for living. It is for felling trees and bringing them into the city to build houses and to fire kilns in which clay bricks can be hardened.

Interestingly, the epic describes this resource extraction and lets us admire the two heroes who undertake it, but the epic also shows that this deed comes with a steep price attached, which takes the form of the gods deciding to punish the two trespassers. Gilgamesh is spared, but Enkidu must die. He suffers a slow and painful death, leaving Gilgamesh heartbroken and unhinged. He doesn't believe that Enkidu is dead until he sees a worm crawling out of his nose— one of the epic's most affective and touching details.

What, in this epic, does an unhinged person do? He leaves the city and roams in the wild. Gilgamesh runs from one end of the world to the other, his clothes in tatters, living on the steppes, as his best friend once did. It's almost as if he is trying to relive Enkidu's life, though in reverse, leaving the city for the wilderness.

Roaming Gilgamesh encounters Utnapishtim at the end of the world, which is where he hears the story of the flood. It isn't what he had come for. He was looking for eternal life but missed his chance; by the end of the epic, he finally returns to Uruk, having made his peace with death. The epic concludes by giving us another tour of the walls, bricks, temples, and clay pits that make the city so great. This is how an epic that defines the difference between humans and animals, civilization and barbarity, has to end: with the triumph of settled life, secured by a wall.

The *Epic of Gilgamesh* is the first important record of human settlement, the mode of life that set us on a path of destabilizing our ecosystem. For this reason, this text offers important clues about how we got here. It also shows how important it is today to read this text, and specifically to read it against the grain, with attention to how our mode of life first emerged, how it has justified itself, and therefore how it might be altered.

What we need in this situation is a new reading of this foundational story, one that does not believe in the wall and recognizes that what sustains the city inside the wall is the resource-rich environment outside of it. It is a reading attuned to what one might term infrastructure, in the broad sense recently suggested by Jedediah Purdy, which includes engineering and agriculture in the context of entire ecosystems.[14] Translated into the terms of the *Epic of Gilgamesh*, infrastructure includes not only the city of Uruk but also the forests of Lebanon as well as the rivers Tigris and Euphrates, which sustain the city's agriculture but also threaten the city with devastating floods.

The environmental reading of the *Epic of Gilgamesh* suggested above is but one example of how the deep history of literature can be seen as so many documents that describe and justify resource extraction in its various forms of development. In fact, I believe that the entire canon of world literature would lend itself to such an investigation. Environmental reading of the kind I propose here doesn't need to cherry-pick specific texts or genres, for example those focused on descriptions of nature. Rather, the claim is that all texts and genres can be subject to an environmental reading because of literature's complicity with the lifestyle that has led to climate change. It is striking how consistently (though variously) literature draws a line between civilization and wilderness once one starts looking for the pattern. Let me provide a few more examples, chosen with a view toward variety.

Moving on from *Gilgamesh*, one might turn to another epic from the ancient world, the *Odyssey*. What comes into focus in this epic is the Cyclopes episode, with its attention to alternative forms of commerce and agriculture. The entire episode amounts to a dismissal of people who don't participate in the Greek world of seaborne trade and its particular form of agriculture.

The negative report on the Cyclopes is told, of course, by Odysseus himself, a shipwrecked sailor trying to find favor with his hosts, on whom his fate now depends. Odysseus is therefore likely to exaggerate the bad treatment he had received from previous hosts. The first description of the Cyclopes frames the episode by focusing on the strange form of agriculture these people practice. "They put their trust in gods, / and do not plant their goods from seed, nor plow. / And yet the barley, grain, and clustering wine-grapes / all flourish there, increased by rain from Zeus."[15] At first blush, this sounds very much like a typical agricultural society, similar perhaps to Mesopotamia, where most of the grains mentioned by Odysseus were first cultivated, sustaining a settled life.

But there is one important difference (important to Odysseus, that is): the Cyclopes grow these agricultural products without having to work for them. This difference is immediately joined by a second—namely, that they lack the political organization typical of Greece: "They hold no councils, have no common laws, / but live in caves on lofty mountain-tops, / and each makes laws for his own wife and children, without concern for what the others think."[16] Odysseus paints a picture of radical isolation, of individual families living by themselves without a sense of community or polity. Once again, it is city dwelling that is privileged here, the kind available in the city-states prevalent in Greece.

The final oddity, in Odysseus's mind, is that the Cyclopes do not participate in maritime trade and instead live in (relative) isolation from the rest of the world. Upon seeing this rich island, Odysseus immediately begins to imagine what could be accomplished here by Greek enterprise, what harbors could be created, what fields plowed, what kind of trade set up. Clearly, the Cyclopes do not know what they could do with their natural resources, do not recognize the full potential of their land. Like Enkidu in the *Epic of Gilgamesh*, they are, somehow, "wild."

With this negative framing concluded, Odysseus proceeds to recount what actually happened here. Once Odysseus and his companions arrive, they find one of the Cyclopes gone but enter the cave anyway. Now begins the riveting drama of the murderous Polyphemus, who disrespects the rules of hospitality (which Odysseus praises his audience for upholding, since his life depends on it), who kills and eats humans (instead of feeding them, like a good host would). This monstrous antihost will have to be brought down through the cunning of Odysseus, who uses a special wine to make him drunk. Once the guest-eating Polyphemus has passed out, Odysseus sharpens a pole, heats it in a fire, and drives it into the Cyclops's single eye.

At this point, the narrative becomes particularly gory. Odysseus describes his revenge with not one but two extended similes, comparing the movement of turning the pole in the eye to a drill used in ship-building (again, the importance of maritime trade and technology) and then the sizzling of the injured eye to that of a blacksmith who puts a red-hot iron in a bucket of water (another technology the Cyclopes do not possess or need). This is what these two similes sound like in Emily Wilson's characteristically direct and powerful rendering:

They took the olive spear, its tip all sharp,
and shoved it in his eye. I leaned on top
and twisted it, as when a man drills wood
for shipbuilding. Below, the workers spin
the drill with straps, stretched out from either end.
So round and round it goes, and so we whirled
the fire-sharp weapon in his eye. His blood
poured out around the stake, and blazing fire
sizzled his lids and brows, and fried the roots.
As when a blacksmith dips an axe or adze
to temper it in ice-cold water; loudly
it shrieks. From this, the iron takes on its power.
So did his eyeball crackle on the spear.[17]

Before inviting us to enjoy this much-anticipated revenge, however, Odysseus has inadvertently provided his listeners with details of Cyclopes living that contradict his framing story. While he had originally presented the Cyclopes as lazy recipients of divine plenitude, we now learn that they actually work very hard for their sustenance. For one thing, Polyphemus is a neat housekeeper: "We saw his crates weighed down with cheese, and pens / crammed full of lambs divided up by age."[18] Everywhere is evidence of careful animal husbandry and agricultural activity, like that surrounding the best of Greek cities. Even the claim that the Cyclopes live in isolation from on another is proven wrong by Odysseus's own words. When the blinded Polyphemus calls for help, help comes immediately. "[He] shouted for the Cyclopes who lived in caves high up on windy cliffs around. / They heard and came from every side, and stood near to the cave, and called out, 'Polyphemus! / What is the matter? Are you badly hurt? / Why are you screaming through the holy night / and keeping us awake? Is someone stealing your herds, or trying to kill you, by some trick or force?'"[19] Clearly, these are not people who live in isolation from each other but a community that rallies immediately to defend one of its members who appears to be in distress. The Cyclopes help one another out; they form a proper society.

Like the *Epic of Gilgamesh*, the *Odyssey* draws a line between civilization and barbarity. The line is similar, if not identical, to the Mesopotamian epic in that it involves agriculture, though here we are dealing not with a grazing wildling but with the odd picture of agriculture and domesticated animal husbandry succeeding allegedly (but not actually) without labor. Equally important is Homer's emphasis on long-distance trade and shipping, the core of the Greek economy, which the Cyclopes lack. This different economic base also explains the diverging attitudes toward the institution of hospitality, which is so central to this episode and the entire epic: hospitality is particularly important for long-distance trade. As subsistence farmers, the Cyclopes do not need hospitality, which is why they are happy to violate its rules.

One could follow the representation of agriculture, animal husbandry, and trade throughout the canon of world literature. The next stop might be Homer's Roman imitator, Virgil. The *Aeneid* is yet another foundational story that revolves around the drama of burning and building urban spaces. Its narrative is like a cord suspended between two cities, beginning with the destruction of Troy and ending with the founding of Rome. To gain a fuller purchase on this epic's attitude toward agriculture, urban living, and other aspects of resource extraction, it should be read side by side with Virgil's other great work, the *Georgics*, which delves deeply into the Roman knowledge-base of agriculture from crop rotation to beekeeping as well as the infrastructure that enabled a city such as Rome to exist in the first place.[20] Held side by side, this pair of texts reveals the relation between city life and agriculture without fully recognizing their interdependence. Emphasizing this interdependence is what an environmental reading would be able to do.

The interplay of an urbanized world with what now appears to be wilderness turns out to be quite important to a number of foundational epics. But there are other genres that could be opened up to this kind of environmental reading, for example the animal fable, which brings select elements of the wilderness into the human world of its readers. As writing increased in the ancient world, more oral stories were written down, especially shorter tales, animal fables among them. These tales were collected and sometimes held together with a framing narrative. Such collections became a widespread genre in the first millennium of the Common Era.

When it comes to animal fables, one the most important collections is the *Panchatantra*, a South Asian text framed as a tool for educating princes. In those fables, speaking animals enact scenes with trenchant morals for the edification of princelings destined to shoulder the burden of kingship. These stories were so successful—less is known about the success of the princelings—that they can be found in many other collections as well. Also from South Asia are the *Jataka Tales*, which are likewise based on animal fables but adapted to a Buddhist worldview with a cunning device: the tales are told by the Buddha, who himself inhabited these animal bodies in earlier incarnations. Animal fables are also included in the *Arabian Nights*, in Aesop's *Fables* (which borrow from Eastern stories), and in many other collections as well. Reading across these texts, one can track how stories morph from one collection, and culture, to the next. Sometimes the same moral is derived, but the animal changes, according to the local fauna of wherever the tale is being told and collected.

What all these fables have in common is that they bring wild animals into the city by means of literature while also assimilating them to human life, above all by giving them speech. In order to read animal fables, we need to interpret them as so many ways of domesticating wilderness, of bringing it into the domain of human sociability, much like Enkidu. Within these stories, animals converse, debate morals, and behave in most ways like humans. More important, they enact human concerns. These concerns are particularly evident if one relates them to the frame tales by which they are held together and which give them purpose, such as the education of princes in the *Panchatantra* or the survival of the storyteller Scheherazade in the case of the *Arabian Nights*. These frame tales betray the true purpose of the stories collected within them, or rather, they impose their own, human, courtly purposes on them.

Turning from story collections to another major genre, the novel, we find that the challenge of reading novels in light of climate change takes a different form. In the first great novel of world literature, the *Tale of Genji*, written by a lady-in-waiting at the Heian court around the year 1000 CE, most of the action takes place within a few city blocks of the capital, and almost all indoors. Exile is seen as the greatest possible punishment, the forcible ejection of a member into the outside world. Hundreds of years later, something similar happens in the important Chinese novel *Dream of the Red Chamber*, which is confined to the interior of a family compound. All hell breaks loose on the rare occasion when someone leaves this enclosed space for the wilderness, urban or otherwise, that surrounds it.

This emphasis of the novel on human sociability is even more pronounced in the modern era. Recently, the novelist Amitav Ghosh has taken to task the realist canon of the modern novel for being too exclusively focused on the social world while neglecting the resource-extracting lifestyle that made that world possible.[21] In order to move beyond this narrow focus, he calls for a broadening and deepening of our reading habits.

I agree with this broadening just as I agree with this characterization of realist fiction, but I don't think this argument implies that we should stop reading realist novels. Rather, the very lack of attention to the environment that is often at work in these novels is something we need to understand through close scrutiny, and that means through a new and different kind of reading (which, after all, is exactly what Gosh does). As with so many other contemporary challenges, what matters is not only *what* we read but also *how* we read. In this sense, environmental reading isn't so different from, say, postcolonial reading that examined realist fiction with attention to the brief moments when colonialism appeared in these works, often in passing. In the case of environmental reading, this includes attention not only to how texts view wilderness, but also to how they assume to have mastered it, not least by dividing the world into conceptual zones of wilderness and settled spaces.

Only very recently has literature sought solace in the wilderness.[22] Texts seeking and praising wilderness are historical exceptions, obscuring the role literature has played in creating a sedentary lifestyle that is now devastating the planet, the extent to which literature, beginning with the *Epic of Gilgamesh*, has contributed to shoring up our defenses, to defining and defending settled living against all possible alternatives.

The conclusion that should be drawn from this argument is that there is no text of world literature which is not also a document of climate change. If we want to understand where our stories about nature come from, which narratives have occupied our minds and sense of self, we must read the entire history of literature in new ways: as texts that track our evolution into sedentary creatures; as narratives that tend to

justify the values that set us on a path toward agricultural life and resource extraction; as stories that
accompany our ingrained habits of thinking and living. We need to recognize these stories in order to
understand the collective choices we have made, if we
are ever to shake loose from them.

CHAPTER TWO

A REVOLUTION
IN ACCOUNTING

READING WORKS OF LITERATURE as documents of resource-extracting life is important, but it is only one aspect of the environmental mode of reading I am trying to sketch. For literature doesn't simply document the choices we have collectively made; it is itself a byproduct of those choices. In other words, literature is not a neutral observer but a deeply compromised participant.

The best way to underscore just how fully literature is entangled with our resource-extracting mode of life is by focusing on its technological dimension, which means the history of writing. It so happens that the best text with which to begin such an analysis is the *Epic of Gilgamesh*. Or rather, it's no accident that this text is both a great document of resource extraction and a text that plays a pivotal role in the development of written literature. The two are deeply and systematically intertwined.

The first full writing system in the world emerged in Mesopotamia's earliest urban spaces, which were made, as the *Epic of Gilgamesh* reminds us, of clay bricks, the marvelous building technology that made urbanism possible. But clay was good for something else besides forming bricks, walls, houses, and, if you were a Mesopotamian god, people like Enkidu: it was good for writing. Cuneiform writing required moist clay onto which three-dimensional incisions could be made before the tablets would be hardened in the sun or, for extra strength, fired in a kiln.

The art of writing, of putting words on clay, is something the *Epic of Gilgamesh* mentions with as much pride as the urban structure of Uruk. After all, it brags that Gilgamesh himself knows how to write. Unlike other early epics such as the Homeric ones, which pretend that they are being sung orally and depict a world in which writing doesn't exist (with one exception, in the case of the *Iliad*), the *Epic of Gilgamesh* delights in being written down.[1]

There is a story about the invention of writing that Mesopotamian scribes recorded to commemorate this formidable invention.[2] It takes place in Uruk, the city so central to the *Epic of Gilgamesh*, and revolves around the rivalry between an early king of Uruk (predecessor of Gilgamesh), King Enmerkar, and the king of neighboring Aratta. Seeking to force Aratta into subservience, Enmerkar sends a messenger with threats of invasion. Unimpressed, Aratta sends the messenger back with a challenge, and so it goes a couple of times: Enmerkar meeting challenges and sending threats,

Aratta rebuffing them and sending more challenges. Finally, Enmerkar is so enraged that he unleashes a long rant against Aratta. The rant creates panic in his trusted messenger, who has been faithfully running between the two kings, because it is too long for him to remember. Confronted with this impasse, Enmerkar takes some clay, puts his words onto the clay, and sends the messenger back to Aratta with the clay tablet. Once the messenger arrives with his new handheld device, the tablet makes such an impression on the king of Aratta that he finally submits.

Two things are interesting about this story. The first is that it highlights the power of writing: a small tablet is more effective than threats of invasion. (Needless to say, this is a self-serving account of writing, written by scribes who want to make sure we understand the potency of their profession.) The other interesting feature is that it has nothing to do with storytelling. The early uses of writing, in Mesopotamia, were similar to the one recorded in the fragment about Enmerkar and Aratta in that they concerned matters of state. Writing was used for record keeping, for building up the first state bureaucracies, and it allowed rulers to project their power farther afield—all the way to Aratta. Ultimately, writing made it possible for city-states to transform themselves into the first territorial empires. It was only hundreds of years after the initial invention of writing that longer written stories such as the early versions of the *Epic of Gilgamesh* emerged. These written stories, too, were used as means of territorial expansion, or at least profited from them, as evidenced by the fragments of the epic that were found all over the Middle East.

The close association of city-states and writing helps explain why the *Epic of Gilgamesh* is so invested in drawing a line between city and wilderness and why this distinction is (so to speak) baked into the underlying technology of writing. When we read the *Epic of Gilgamesh* with respect to environmental matters, we are therefore dealing with a deeply complicit form of expression. This is also the reason why literature has tended, until very recently, to be on the side of urbanism, sedentary life, the division of labor, and of states.

For our purposes, the complicity of literature with urban living and resource extraction is not necessarily a bad thing. The *Epic of Gilgamesh* shows the extent to which literature is one of the many by-products of settled life and that it has shaped our understanding of how humans should live, what they should eat, which resources they should use, and what they should do if they encounter beings who refuse this order (the unfortunate answer is that such beings should either be killed, like Humbaba, blinded, like Polyphemus, or seduced into settled life, like Enkidu).

After writing was invented in Mesopotamia as a by-product of city life and as a vehicle for exporting city-based values into the hinterland (now designated as wilderness), this technology spread to other early cultures such as Egypt, Assyria, and China. They all had in common a developed agricultural life that allowed for a new division of labor, requiring a new cast of scribes to keep track of produce, sales, and state governance. These scribes were the original white-collar accountants.

The various early writing cultures also had in common that they were located on a single landmass: the Eurasian continent. It is possible, thought difficult to prove, that the idea of writing, so vividly described in the story of Uruk and Aratta, was invented only once and then spread to other early writing cultures such as Egypt and China. This would mean that literature as we know it was the product of a single inspiration.

There exists, however, a second, completely independent, origin of writing in Mesoamerica. When Hernán Cortés arrived in Yucatán, in what is today southern Mexico, equipped not only with cannons and steel but also with his newly printed Bibles, Johannes Gutenberg having recently reinvented the Chinese technology of print, he encountered a culture that had been completely isolated from Eurasia for thousands of years and that had invented writing—and literature—all on its own. This, for me, is one of the most astonishing results of large-scale comparative thinking about literature. The rich history of Maya literature is still almost entirely unknown outside a narrow circle of experts, even though it is now 1,500 years old.

Maya literature is unique in that it is the only completely separate literary tradition in the world. Even though the Spaniards following Cortés did their best to eradicate Maya books, some of these works survived, above all the epic *Popol Vuh*.[3] Mesoamerica is like a control experiment in literature to gauge what would happen if there existed a society that developed literature without contact with any other literate culture. Intriguingly, the Maya experiment returns the same results as Eurasia: the *Popol Vuh* is deeply aware of its agricultural base, and particularly elevates maize as the society's main crop.

The *Popol Vuh* includes an account of the creation of humans, one that is more elaborate than the ones offered in many other epics, in that humans are successfully created only on the fourth try. A first attempt yields not humans but the animals of the forest, who can't speak and are therefore a grave disappointment to their makers.[4] Undeterred, the gods continue their work and create beings out of earth and mud. But the resulting creatures are misshapen, can't talk in comprehensible ways, and finally dissolve in water.[5] The failure of this (second) experiment stands in contrast to Mesopotamian creation myths as well as one of the two creation stories in the Hebrew Bible where humans are (successfully) created from earth and clay. Apparently, clay was less important to Maya civilization, which makes sense in that its most important buildings and temples were made not from clay bricks but from stone (which is why many of them still stand).

With the failure of the clay experiment, the gods move on to another malleable material: wood from the coral tree. This time, things work out much better in that the carefully carved creatures look and speak like humans. But before long it becomes clear that they lack crucial abilities, above all memory and reason. Despite these failings, the wood-carved people spread out over the earth until they end up being wiped out in a flood. Today, only monkeys are a reminder of this (third) unsuccessful attempt at creation.[6]

As if tired of recounting these repeated acts of making humans, the *Popol Vuh* now turns its attention elsewhere, telling stories about mythical demigods descending into the underworld to play a dangerous ball game against the gods and about trickster twins who outwit their divine adversaries. It is only in the penultimate section of the epic that the theme of creation is picked up again, and this time things finally work out: the first "mother-fathers," as they are called, are made, and fortunately they speak, they have reason, and they last. What has made the difference? It was all in the material: this time, the gods used maize.

The epic goes into some detail:

And then the yellow corn and white corn were ground, and Xmucane did the grinding nine times. Food was used, along with the water she rinsed her hands with, for the creation of grease; it became human fat when it was worked by the Bearer, Begetter, Sovereign Plumed Serpent, as they are called. After that, they put it into words:

the making, the modeling of our first mother-father,
with yellow corn, white corn alone for the flesh,
food alone for the human legs and arms,
for our first fathers, the four human works.
It was staples alone that made up their flesh.[7]

Maize brings about a miracle of creation: this plant yields rich seeds that can be ground up—it has to be done nine times, though—and combined with water to produce human flesh. Maize is miraculous, but it is also ordinary, the main staple of Maya agriculture. White maize and yellow maize, both specified in this creation story, made it possible for the Maya to feed large cities, with their imposing pyramid-shaped temples, such as those located at Palenque and many other sites. Recent infrared images have revealed that the network of settlements and towns, much of them fueled by maize, was much larger than previously assumed, which means that archaeologists are still rediscovering the full extent of classical Maya civilization, much of it hidden below the thick canopy of jungle in Chiapas and Guatemala.

And then, rather suddenly, this sophisticated and impressive urban civilization comes crashing down.

The largest cities are abandoned, the temples crumble and become ruins that are quickly reclaimed by the jungle. Life returns to a less dense, less urban mode, with most Maya surviving in smaller settlements and villages. The reason for this rapid decline, which occurred many centuries before the arrival of the Spaniards, is still not entirely clear, but one likely candidate is the collapse in the production of maize, perhaps due to monoculture and overcultivation.[8] The *Popol Vuh* sides with settled life every bit as much as the *Epic of Gilgamesh*, even though it doesn't address the environmental requirements of city living quite as explicitly.

The collapse was significant, but not absolute. One of the achievements that endured beyond the most urban phase of Maya culture was writing itself, cultivated continually until the arrival of the Spaniards. At this point, a second, more radical decline set in, first through a civil war instigated by Spanish conquistadors, then through smallpox brought by them, and finally through increasing Spanish settlement, which decimated the Maya population and forced the survivors into indentured labor and servitude.[9]

The Spaniards also brought along Franciscans, who sometimes protested the worst abuses of colonization but who also wanted to convert the Maya. At first, Franciscans thought that conversion worked surprisingly well until they realized that the Maya simply placed the new Christian god alongside older ones.[10]

Enraged, the Franciscans decided to take out the older gods and rituals by their roots. But what were the roots of these old beliefs? The so-called Council Books, in which the stories of the Maya were written down in their distinct glyphs, which function a bit like Egyptian hieroglyphs. The glyphs were written on a kind of paper and the pages bound accordion-style. There were not many such books, which is why they were precious possessions passed down within families, but the Spaniards tracked them down and burnt them whenever they could.[11] Having become very thorough when it came to destroying pagan gods, the Franciscans got almost all of the Maya books.

At this point, the few remaining Maya scribes were faced with a terrible dilemma. Their world had been overrun by foreign soldiers, pestilence, and priests, and their books had gone up in flames. They observed knowledge of their precious writing system declining rapidly. Would their writing culture survive at all?

Three surviving scribes made a cunning but also depressing decision. They wanted to preserve their stories, including the story of the creation of humans from maize, so that those stories would be read in the future. But knowing that that future would most likely not include knowledge of the difficult Maya glyphs, they decided to write in the Latin alphabet, the writing system of the victors.[12] This was how the *Popol Vuh* came to be written down, in secret, and preserved, despite the destructive rage unleashed against Maya writing and storytelling. It is only because of these three anonymous scribes that we have available, for our own purposes today, a great and unique epic, one deeply entangled with its own agricultural base.

The flipside of the history of writing sketched above, from Eurasia to the Americas, is the continuing importance of orality. It would be inaccurate to imagine the spread of writing as a process by which writing gradually replaced orality. Instead, each new revolution in writing technology—such as those brought by paper, papyrus, and parchment, the new writing formats such as tablets, scrolls, and books, and finally by Chinese woodblock printing and Gutenberg's assembly-line production of printed books—changed the relation between writing and orality. Writing and orality are like a dyad or an equation: change one element, and you also change the other.

One of the best example of the enduring force of orality in the midst of literacy is the West African *Epic of Sunjata*. It commemorates an empire that existed in the late Middle Ages, roughly in today's Mali, led by King Sunjata. His story does not begin auspiciously since he is born with severe disabilities, unable to walk upright, the result of a curse uttered by a rival. When he is strong enough to overcome this handicap by throwing off the curse, his mother takes him into exile to save him from the murderous intentions of his rivals. Thus begins a long period of exile during which young Sunjata and his mother are vagrants, cast out from their settled place, roaming the world, sometimes pitied and sometimes assaulted but always dependent on strangers. It is only after many years of exile that Sunjata is called back, his country much weakened by war. He must prove his worth in a series of battles before he can take his rightful place.

The *Epic of Sunjata* is a story not about the glories of settled life but about the inverse: the pains of not having a home. It is closer in this respect to the *Odyssey* than to the *Epic of Gilgamesh*, though the latter also includes a period in which grieving Gilgamesh is roaming the world in despair. Consequently, in the *Epic of Sunjata* there is less emphasis on the agricultural base of settled urbanism.

Sometimes, however, agriculture does seep in through the cracks just as it does in Homer. There is a crucial scene in which the emissaries from home make contact with Sunjata, hiding in exile, with his small entourage (his mother has since died). The exiles yearn for food from home, especially *dado*, dried hibiscus blossoms used as a condiment in a particular sauce.[13] The two emissaries from home have brought some *dado* to sell in the market. When the exiles see the *dado*, they yearn so much for it that they simply take it without so much as bargaining for it beforehand, right there in the middle of the crowded market. Based on this telltale sign, contact between them and Sunjata is established. For *dado* is not produced here, in exile. It is specific to home.

Stories of Sunjata and his empire were transmitted orally for centuries—even after Arab scholars had introduced Islam and its writing culture to sub-Saharan Africa. The epic received something of an Islamic veneer in that Islam and Islamic book learning are evoked in the epic, though much of the pre-Islamic material remained intact.[14]

When French colonists arrived in the nineteenth century, they brought along their own alphabet and writing culture, but yet again the epic continued to be told orally alongside the new centers of power, bureaucracy, and education. It was transformed into writing only over the course of the twentieth century, through a process that involved much trial and error.[15] First was an attempt to turn the epic into a five-act play (modeled on French drama), then came the idea to turn it into a novel (modeled on the French midcentury novel). None of these genres worked well with the material, shaped by generations of storytellers, and so the epic of Sunjata continued to be recited orally, as it still is today.

I had the good fortune of working with David C. Conrad, who collaborated with a Mande singer, Tassey Condé, to produce what I consider the best written version of the epic: a rendering based on live sessions recorded in 1994 that Conrad then translated into English and shaped into a written epic in the late twentieth and early twenty-first centuries.[16]

This ongoing exchange between writing and orality is a reminder that the spread of writing leads all too easily to a dismissal of oral traditions, whereas writing and orality should be studied together, as a single system. There is much work to be done in the recovery of oral knowledge, which is often found outside traditional centers of written culture, as well as in Native communities (though those communities also have significant traditions of print).[17] Fortunately, ecocriticism and anthropology have been very active in the area, with a focus on different traditions of memory and storytelling, which can also be used to reconstruct past environmental disasters whose effects were preserved in oral story tradition, for example in the western United States.[18]

A reflection on the history of writing provides the ground on which to gauge literature's complicity with sedentary life and resource extraction. It measures how deeply and to what extent literature, as a cultural technique, is interwoven with the history that has caused climate change. The purpose of this kind of history is not to denounce literature as it has been written down for the past four thousand years but to develop a mode of reading suitable to the task at hand: understanding the types of thinking and storytelling that got us into the situation we're in today. Reading environmentally will allow us to seize four thousand years of literature and use it for our own purposes, which is nothing less than to redefine our relation to the environment.

CHAPTER THREE

THE TWO FACES OF WORLD LITERATURE

THE TASK OF REREADING foundational texts of human history with an eye toward climate change involves zooming in on how individual texts—and scenes within texts—describe and justify human intervention in the ecosystem, but it also involves zooming out and considering hundreds or even thousands of years of literature in order to perceive patterns over time, as sketched in the readings above. It is the latter, the zooming out, that is much less practiced in literary study, which is why I now want to make explicit an argument that underpins what I have outlined so far, namely an argument in favor of large-scale perspectives.

A convenient approach to large-scale thinking and reading is provided by the concept of *world literature*. I suggest this term because world literature is the subfield of literary studies that cuts across narrow boundaries of time and space and understands human storytelling as occurring on an interconnected, global scale, which in turn allows for broad, cross-cultural comparisons. Equally important, world literature captures the deep history of storytelling, from orality and the first written epics to the mass-produced literature of the industrial age, a history that is important for understanding how complicit literature is with our resource-extracting way of life.

Another way of saying this is that the term *world literature* focuses our minds on the world itself. When I read world literature, I always find myself thinking about how a work survived, how it traveled from its point of origin into my hands, who translated it, and who published it. In this sense, world literature is a worldly approach to literature, one that is engaged in cultural infrastructure; in technologies such as the alphabet, paper, or print; in institutions such as temples and libraries; in modes of cultural exchange (both violent and peaceful); and in education. It is this worldly focus of world literature that now makes it the key to the storytelling species that we are, and the key to learning something useful from its history for our changing planet.

Where did the idea of world literature come from? Surprisingly, perhaps, it emerged very recently, less than two hundred years ago. It is worth zooming in on one moment of origin, because this moment reveals both how useful the term can be now but also how compromised it is, how much it, too, needs to be read against the grain if it is to be informed by climate change.[1] To arrive at such a reading, I will pay minute attention to the motivation of the actors involved, their fears, hopes, and implicit assumptions.

The scene I have in mind is a conversation that involved two people, who met, not for the first time, on January 31 in the year 1827 in the small, provincial town of Weimar. One of them was Johann Wolfgang von Goethe, seventy-seven years of age, and at the height of his fame as one of Europe's foremost poets. Ralph Waldo Emerson would soon count him as one of the seven representative men of all time, among such luminaries as Plato, Shakespeare, and Napoleon.[2]

Goethe had grown up in the cosmopolitan city of Frankfurt and become an overnight sensation with the publication of *The Sorrows of Young Werther*, a novel based on a love triangle that taught an entire generation how to revel in impossible love, complete with dress code and letters studded with exclamation marks! From the heights of his early success, Goethe had been lured to the deep provinces by the duke of Saxe-Weimar, who gave him the title of privy councilor. Goethe made himself indispensable and was soon put in charge of everything from the court theater to road construction, while continuing to build his literary reputation with novels, plays, poetry, and letters. As a reward, the duke gave him a nice house right in the center of town.

The other participant in the encounter was much younger, thirty-five years of age, and completely obscure.[3] Johann Peter Eckermann had grown up in abject poverty; the family depended on a single cow, and sometimes young Eckermann would accompany his father to peddle small trinkets. He left school early to take a job, but he exhibited an unusual desire for learning. Laboriously he acquired Latin, which enabled him to go back to school, though he was much older than the other pupils. Finally, after surmounting many additional obstacles, he was able to enter the University of Göttingen to study law. He was nearing thirty, but he was on a path of upward mobility.

It was around this time that someone gave him Goethe's works to read, and Eckermann was hooked. Instead of continuing with his legal studies, he composed a dissertation on Goethe's poetry and found the courage to send it to the master himself. He also indicated that he would like to work as his assistant. Too impatient to wait for a response, Eckermann decided to follow the letter in person. Because he was much too poor for a coach, he walked, just as he used to walk with his father when growing up, and arrived in Weimar three weeks later. Goethe was delighted with this helpful newcomer and Eckermann stayed, coming over to Goethe's house several times a week to assist with research, writing, advice, or simply by lending a sympathetic ear.

These were the two protagonists, then, who came together on January 31, 1827, as they had innumerable times in the preceding years, a Wednesday. As usual,

Goethe started to report on his recent thoughts and experiences, and mentioned that he had been reading a Chinese novel. "Really? That must have been rather strange!" Eckermann responded.[4] Goethe was having none of it. "Much less so than one thinks," he declared, to the great astonishment of Eckermann. Clearly, Eckermann had never thought about Chinese novels and didn't know what to expect. But Goethe was inspired by his reading experience and observed how morally superior this novel was compared to so much of the literature then in fashion in Paris. Eckermann, now slowly catching on, tried to say something good about this novel at last: "Isn't it strange that the works of this Chinese writer are so morally elevated while those of the foremost poet of France [meaning Pierre-Jean de Béranger] aren't?" This remark was more to Goethe's liking, and he heartily agreed. But Eckermann couldn't keep up the façade of being a lover of Chinese novels and let it slip that the novel Goethe had been reading must have been unusually good, an exception to the rule. Once again, Goethe reprimanded his assistant: "Nothing could be further from the truth. The Chinese have thousands of them, and had them when our ancestors were still living in the woods." Not content with this riposte, Goethe went one step further, drawing a wild conclusion: "The era of world literature is at hand, and everyone must contribute to accelerating it."

This articulation of the idea of world literature is unusual in that we know exactly how it happened. The reason is Eckermann's poverty—and Goethe's parsimony. Even though Goethe had accepted Eckermann's services, he paid his assistant very little for his troubles, which meant that Eckermann had to think of an additional source of income. At some point the idea hit him to record his weekly conversations with one of Europe's most famous writers. Surely, there would be a market for that? He mentioned the idea to Goethe, and Goethe permitted him to take notes; unfortunately, he also asked that Eckermann wait to publish them until after Goethe's death. Eckermann, still hard-pressed for funds, acquiesced and dutifully took notes on their conversations, mostly after the fact, including the conversation of January 31, 1827.

What does this birth of world literature have to do with how we tell the story of human history and its relation to the environment? At first blush very little, but there is more here than meets the eye. What informed the conversation between Goethe and Eckermann was what we would call globalization. Just before using the term *world literature*, Goethe had declared nationalism over: "National literatures don't mean much anymore. The era of world literature is at hand, and everyone must contribute to accelerating it." In 1827, declaring the end of nationalism was a daring statement because the nineteenth century was a high tide of nationalism, especially in Germany, which had not yet achieved national unification and was divided into small and medium-sized kingdoms and duchies such as the one of Saxe-Weimar. All around Goethe, writers were busy discovering German folktales and building national traditions, trying to create a sense of nationhood, through culture, that was not yet tenable politically.

Goethe disliked nationalism because he realized that national silos create arbitrary divisions between cultures. Most writers read across centuries and cultures almost naturally, even when their reading habits weren't nearly as wide as Goethe wished. This was why he was constantly seeking literature his contemporaries disregarded, from Chinese novels to Sanskrit dramas and Persian poetry.

Despite the prevalence of nationalism, Goethe knew that he lived during a time of expanding cultural horizons as European colonialism and international trade were forcing different parts of the world into closer contact, with far-reaching consequences. One of those consequences concerned literature: for the first time in human history, it was possible for someone like him, stuck in a provincial German town, to gain access to an incredibly broad array of literature. Whether the nationalists around him liked it or not, market realities were accelerating the cultural exchange among nations. World literature was the result of a growing world market in literature.

Goethe recognized that translation was one of the forces that fueled this process of globalization. Even though he spent significant time learning languages—

he took up Arabic at an advanced age—he knew that he could not possibly learn all the languages whose literature he was eager to read. Only three Chinese novels had been translated into European languages, one by an agent of the East India Company, a reminder that European colonialism was one of the forces bringing different parts of the world into closer contact. World literature was not pure or untainted by these historical forces; it was a by-product of them.[5]

Even though questions of globalization, nationalism, and empire dominated the birth of world literature (as an idea or concept), there also exists an intriguing and lesser-known environmental backstory to Goethe's coinage. This backstory involves Goethe's fascination with geology and biology, both of which were connected to his practice as a writer and reader. World literature, as conceived of by Goethe, derived not only from a new understanding of literature, but also from a new understanding of the world.

The close association of literature, geology, and botany is visible in the experience that shaped Goethe's mature years more than any other: his travels to Italy. Goethe's yearning for Italy originated in his reading of Roman literature, but once he arrived in Italy, he was particularly eager to proceed to Sicily because the island had been a significant Greek colony. Given the constraints on his time—he had had to sneak away from Weimar in secret, informing only his butler and the duke—Goethe knew that Sicily was going to be as close to Greek antiquity as he was ever going to get.

Goethe's months in Sicily were months immersed in Greek literature.[6] He reread Homer's *Odyssey*, in part because several of its episodes might have been set in and around the island, and started working on a tragedy based on the Nausicaa episode of the epic, when Odysseus is shipwrecked and taken up by Princess Nausicaa and her father, King Alcinous. "There is no better commentary on the *Odyssey* than being in this environment," he noted excitedly in his travelogue.[7]

Goethe's immersion in Greek literature was accompanied by a renewed interest in a long-standing obsession: finding the original plant, or *Urpflanze*. Not content with the prevailing classification of plants proposed by Linnaeus, Goethe had developed the idea that there must have been an original plant from which all others were derived. By observing and drawing plants and studying their varieties, he hoped to reduce their form to a single prototype. Periodically, he went searching for such a plant in botanical gardens, which is why the botanical garden of Palermo, in Sicily, caught his attention, leading him to spend several days there instead of visiting the city's palaces and other architectural highlights.

Goethe, who liked to find similarities across different domains, applied a similar model to literature. It was an evolutionary model in the sense that it had to do with original forms, prototypes that were the original building blocks from which all other, later versions were ultimately derived. This was one reason why he was so interested in early literatures, including when Greek literature moved from orality to literature, but also other early literatures such as Sanskrit. Learning about origins, according to Goethe's presumption, would teach him something about the essence of a thing, be it plants or works of literature.

It wasn't just the *Urpflanze* that was on Goethe's mind while he dug deep into the origins of Greek literature. He also took an interest in the island's geology, frequently straying from the path to examine rock formations and riverbeds. Goethe lived before geologists developed the theory of tectonic plates, just as he lived before the theory of evolution, but he sensed that human activity, including the writing of stories, should be understood as unfolding within an environment that ranged from geological formations to plants and animals. This was the second way that an incipient environmental thinking entered Goethe's conception of the world, not only as a morphology of origins but also as an attention to the shaping power of the environment, broadly construed.

When Goethe talked about world literature decades later, he brought these two dimensions, the interest in the *Urpflanze* and the interest in the environment, together.

Goethe's interest in geology and botany took place in the context of a rapidly changing awareness of just how complex and interconnected different parts of the world really were. Goethe's main source for this insight was a personal acquaintance, Alexander von Humboldt. In recent years, Humboldt has been rediscovered as a pioneer of environmental science; his biographer Andrea Wulf credits him with nothing less than having invented nature.[8] The claim is not as exaggerated as it sounds, provided that by nature we mean a finely calibrated, interconnected whole.

Humboldt came by this idea honestly, which is to say, through travel. While Goethe had traveled only in western and southern Europe, Humboldt traveled as often as he could and as far as his funds would allow, all the way to Russia in the east and the Americas in the west. This range was crucial because it allowed him to compare flora and fauna across continents and climate zones. His most surprising finding was that climate zones cut across continents, producing similar results across vast distances. He captured this view in his famous *Naturgemälde*, extraordinary cross sections of mountains that traverse different climate zones vertically, whose composition Humboldt then compared to those in other parts of the world, vertically.

The picture Humboldt painted was different from Goethe's *Urpflanze*. While Goethe wanted to trace the shapes of plants back to a single origin, Humboldt was interested in correspondences, in how similar climatic environments produce similar results. Both theories would undergo significant revision with Charles

FIGURE 1. *Naturgemälde*, or nature painting, by Alexander von Humboldt, showing a mountain traversing different climate zones.

Darwin's theory of evolution, which can be understood as a combination of the two: like Goethe, Darwin was interested in prototypes, in following different types to their original forms; and, like Humboldt, he was interested in the shaping power of the environment.

Neither Goethe nor Humboldt fully articulated the relation between globalization and environmental thinking, though both seem to have sensed a connection. Of the two writers, Humboldt was probably more aware of this connection, since he was fighting against nationalism as well as colonialism and slavery, which he encountered on his travels across the Americas, from the Andes to the United States (where he met with Jefferson), while also developing his new vision of ecology. It seems that his view of nature as a finely tuned ecosystem extended to humans. Their actions, he knew, occurred within the complicated mesh that he captured in his *Naturgemälde*. For Goethe, the two domains, economic globalization and environmental thinking, remained more separate, leaving it to us to do the work of connecting them.

I have always found the connection between globalization and ecology, which I think of as the two faces of world literature, intriguing and underexplored. Both Goethe and Humboldt had a finely tuned appreciation for differences, different cultures but also different ecosystems, both of which, they knew, required a great deal of humility to be understood. They also both sensed that, for all the importance attributed to difference, human cultures were part of an integrated whole just as human life existed in a much larger environment.

Others in Goethe's orbit developed similar ideas with respect to what one might call the ecology of culture. Humboldt's brother, Wilhelm, pursued a lifelong interest in the evolution of languages, drawing elaborate language trees. Johann Gottfried von Herder related the study of language families to different folk cultures from around the world. Like Wilhelm von Humboldt, he was also a student of translation, which Goethe saw as central to the circulation of literature beyond its origins, enabling him and others to read such works as Chinese novels. Another associate, Friedrich Schelling, who developed his own version of world literature, was a student of Indian literature, inspiring Goethe to read *Shakuntala*, the classical Sanskrit play by the poet Kalidasa (Goethe would incorporate one element of this play, a prelude about theater, into his own *Faust*). Yet another figure, Madame de Staël, would go on to invent the discipline of comparative literature.[9]

What these various thinkers were working on, collectively, was something like the cultural equivalent of Humboldt's *Naturgemälde*, a sense that literature and culture should be studied not only historically, across time, but also laterally, across cultures. Such a broad, comparative approach would result in something that might be called *Kulturgemälde*, a picture of culture as an integrated whole. It was this idea that Goethe would capture, or at least glimpse, while talking to his startled secretary, giving it the name world literature.

This environmental dimension of world literature is important for us now, as we look back at the birth scene of world literature from the vantage point of climate change. This vantage point reveals two different conceptions of *the* world: one is a notion of globalization driven by economic forces that directly affect literature as well; the other is an incipient planetary consciousness that we know is crucial to solving climate change. For Goethe—and for Humboldt—the two notions of world existed next to each other. For us, they are in tension, with economic globalization, in the wake of European colonialism, accelerating the resource-extracting way of life that is destroying our planet. Disentangling these two competing notions of "world" in the term *world literature* is one of the tasks for critical reading practices today.

Yet it is not only the two notions of "world" that need to be examined critically; the same is true of "literature." Here, the complicity of world literature with economic globalization and European colonialism should be seen as the most recent example of literature's complicity with the resource-extracting sedentary way of life that began in Mesopotamia thousands of years ago and accelerated in the wake of colonialism and industrialization.[10] Writing, as we were able to glimpse in the *Epic of Gilgamesh*, was invented by accountants, wielded by the first state bureaucracies, further developed by priests, and remained firmly in the hands of a tiny elite for the first two thousand years of literature, roughly half its existence. But even as writing became available to somewhat larger populations, literacy remained tightly controlled, unavailable to most. Access to literacy and the question of whose stories are told in writing and circulate widely remain a live issue today.

All this is to say that world literature, as invented by Goethe, is a hugely influential but also a deeply compromised idea. Yet this is not a reason to reject it. On the contrary, the tensions at work in this idea, and the complicity of which they speak, are the very reasons why studying literature through the lens of world literature is so crucial with respect to climate change. The perspective offered by world literature will not give us a vantage point from outside sedentary life, or resource extraction, or colonialism, untainted and pure. Such a vantage point would not be helpful, even if it were possible. Complicity is our (analytical) friend because it allows us to study the mechanisms we want to critique.

The tension between the two notions of "world"—economic globalization and its environmental consequences—continue to be visible in the subsequent history of world literature. It took twenty-one years for the term to receive its second prominent billing, in London, in 1848. The question of nationalism was still central, but an environmental dimension was moving into view more clearly:

> By exploiting the world market, the bourgeoisie has made production and consumption a cosmopolitan affair. [. . .] Industries no longer use local materials but raw material drawn from the remotest zones, and its products are consumed not only at home, but also in every quarter of the globe. In place of the old local and national seclusion and self-sufficiency, we have commerce in every direction, universal interdependence of nations. And as in material, so also in intellectual production. The intellectual creations of individual nations become common property. National one-sidedness and narrow-mindedness become increasingly impossible, and from the numerous national and local literatures there arises a world literature.[11]

The authors of this paragraph, Karl Marx and Friedrich Engels, called their text *The Communist Manifesto*. Their paragraph is surprising, perhaps, because it seems to delight in the productive forces unleashed by globalization. Clearly, Marx and Engels have little interest in national one-sidedness and narrow-mindedness and invite everyone to do away with it, even if they be the agents of the bourgeoisie, which is their term for capitalism (the word *capitalism* does not appear in the *Communist Manifesto*). It is only later in the story that the two authors will turn the tables on the world market by seeking to change its rules.

Goethe, the aristocrat who enjoyed the patronage of his duke, would have been surprised to see his term used by two sworn revolutionaries, but he would not have been surprised to see world literature mentioned in the company of global supply chains, given his attention to the market in literature. He might also have sympathized with the environmental dimension of the diagnosis offered by Marx and Engels, who speak of raw materials and mining, of industrialization that is not only remaking social relations but the environment as well. Engels in particular was aware of this dimension, having studied the effects of industrialization in Manchester.

FIGURE 2. Crompton, near Manchester, England, during the height of industrialization.

It is worth noting that Marx and Engels wrote in favor of industrialization and globalization, international supply chains, and resource extraction, just as they wrote in favor of world literature. While the two authors wanted to change capitalism, they also wanted to hold onto the productive forces unleashed by resource extraction and the worldwide exchange of ideas made possible by it.[12]

Neither Goethe nor Marx and Engels could have predicted that the new world market, of which world literature now formed a small part, was beginning to change the climate, steeply accelerating a process that had begun in earnest with the agricultural lifestyle ten thousand years ago. Our challenge, then, is to bring to the fore the environmental dimension of the concept of world literature and to connect it to the history of resource extraction that accelerated in the industrial age.

After Goethe, Marx, and Engels, the term *world literature* became more widely used in different locations and for different purposes. It was most commonly invoked by those hoping to promote literary traditions they felt were not given their due. One of them was Melech Ravitsh, who advocated on behalf of a Yiddish world literature as part of his campaign to increase awareness of Yiddish as a literary language. In South Asia, Rabindranath Tagore used the term to talk about the great Indian epics, the *Ramayana* and the *Mahabharata*, while the Chinese scholar Zheng

Zhenduo was interested in how Chinese literature was perceived abroad.

Despite these differences, there was one theme running through this heterogeneous group: a rejection of nationalism. This rejection also connected this second group to the founders of the term, from Goethe, who had opposed nationalism on cultural grounds, to Marx and Engels, who opposed it on economic and political ones. Ravitsh knew that Yiddish was a language without a nation, spoken and written all over the world (the Jewish national movement was going to favor Hebrew as a national language), and Tagore urged his readers to reject nationalism when fighting against the British Empire.[13]

Zhen Zhenduo not only rejected nationalism in literature but also traced it to the organization of literature departments, bemoaning the fact that universities defined literature, in 1922, along national lines.[14] He would have been surprised—or perhaps gratified in his analysis—to find that the same is true today, one hundred years later. Even though we clearly live in an era of world literature, the study of literature in schools and universities is still based on narrow, nationalist canons, perhaps unsurprisingly so, given that nationalism is resurgent across the world (more surprising is the fact that this arrangement is maintained by humanities scholars who otherwise reject nationalism).

The organization of literature departments along national lines makes it doubly difficult to approach storytelling on the level of world literature, which is all the more deplorable since climate change cannot be solved, or even be understood, as long as we remain tethered to the nation-state.

CHAPTER FOUR

HOW TO ANTHOLOGIZE THE WORLD

IF WORLD LITERATURE IS to be opened up for new, environmental reading practices, where might scholars and writers find access to such a vast and seemingly unmanageable body of work, discouraged as it is by the national organization of literature departments in most parts of the world? One convenient place are world literature anthologies. In many ways, they provide a direct answer to the question: What is world literature? (It was the experience of editing an anthology of world literature that prompted David Damrosch to write a book called *What Is World Literature?*, a classic in the field.) I recommend this path also because it happens to be how I became acquainted with world literature, quite by accident.

It is worth noting that while anthologies have existed for a long time, they have thrived particularly in the postwar American university. They arrived here in the wake of another moment of extreme nationalism, the rise of the Nazis in Germany, which led to an exodus of writers and scholars from Europe to the United States. Among them were two professors of literature, Erich Auerbach and Leo Spitzer. Initially, the two scholars ended up in Istanbul, an indispensable experience that also, quite likely, saved their very lives. From Istanbul, they both moved to the United States, bringing their conception of world literature with them.[1]

Unexpectedly, the idea fell on fertile soil here. As America moved into the postwar era, it experienced an unprecedented expansion of higher education, driven in part by the G.I. Bill, which allowed returning soldiers to attend university for free. This expansion meant that higher education was no longer restricted to a small elite. New populations of students demanded new ways of teaching. It was no longer possible to assume that all students had gone through the same kind of training, with the result that new introductory and general education courses sprung up everywhere. World literature anthologies emerged to fill this pedagogical niche, namely, to provide these students and teachers with a canon of texts and the pedagogical apparatus necessary for reading and teaching it.

Anthologies of world literature don't usually pinpoint explicit environmental themes, but they adopt a big-picture view, allowing their readers access to works that have proved to be influential: stories that accompanied, reflected, defended, and shaped our sedentary, resource-extracting lifestyle. World literature anthologies can be so valuable in uncovering the underlying stories that have kept most of humanity hooked on resource extraction—precisely when they are not presented as environmental anthologies—provided that they are read accordingly.

Anthologies are also useful for studying changes in literary canons. When it comes to using literary history for thinking about climate change, we are not only creating a new canon of environmental literature but also reading past and present canons differently. This doesn't mean that canons should be simply accepted as a given. In fact, they change all the time, so it would make sense that this would also be true during our epoch of climate change, which has already witnessed an emerging canon of environmental literature, mostly centered on the last two centuries. World literature anthologies are a good place to watch canon formation unfold.

The dynamics of canon formation become visible when we compare today's canon as represented in world literature anthologies with the canon envisioned by Goethe two hundred years ago. Some of the texts he promoted, from Chinese novels to Sanskrit drama and Persian poetry, are still staples of world literature, and to this extent, his vision can be seen as a successful act of advocacy.

At the same time, many of the texts that today form the canon of world literature were not even available

FIGURE 3. Rococo Hall of the Anna Amalia Library in Weimar, where Goethe did some of his research on world literature.

to Goethe in the local Anna Amalia library that he helped oversee—one of his many administrative duties. The reason was that in the early nineteenth century, the worldwide circulation of literature as we now tend to take it for granted had barely begun. It was only in the two centuries since Goethe's coinage that many of the texts of world literature were discovered or translated for the first time.

When Goethe explored Chinese literature, for example, the most canonical Chinese novels, *The Journey to the West* and *Dream of the Red Chamber*, had not been translated yet. The same was true of several of the other texts I have mentioned, including the *Epic of Gilgamesh*, which was still buried underneath the rubble of Ashurbanipal's library, the *Tale of Genji*, which did not yet circulate outside Japan, the *Popol Vuh*, which was still languishing in a library, all but forgotten, and the *Epic of Sunjata*, which had not yet been written down and was instead transmitted orally, as the Homeric epics had been for centuries. What is necessary, then, is to update Goethe's canon and then to read this new canon in light of climate change.

My suggestion that we might use world literature anthologies as critical tools is also, as I have mentioned, personal, in that it's how I first got introduced to the big-picture kind of thinking about literature. It happened when I was asked, about fifteen years ago, to step in as general editor of the *Norton Anthology of World Literature*. I have since come to appreciate what anthologies can do and consider it worth dwelling on their history and purpose, an underresearched topic.[2] So please allow me a brief moment of intellectual autobiography.

At first, the category of "world literature" seemed hopelessly daunting. Very quickly I realized that I didn't even know how much I didn't know, how much literature there was that I had never even heard of (including, it pains me to admit, the *Panchatantra*, the *Jataka Tales*, the *Popol Vuh*, and the *Epic of Sunjata*). Panic set in. How could I ever wrap my head around something as large as world literature? Desperate, I began looking for books that would give me guidance.

The first group of texts I read were on world history, which I quickly discovered was a thriving field, with works that tried to synthesize and distill, compare and contrast, and, above all, tried to tell an overall story of humankind. This genre ranged from the scholarly to the popular, but in either approach its task was to think about the broad contours of history, to pinpoint historical forces and agents.[3] I was intrigued by commodity histories such as the ones offered by Mark Kurlansky in *Cod: A Biography of the Fish That Changed the World* (1998) and *Big Oyster: History of the Half-Shell* (2006), which he seasoned with *Salt: A World History* (2002). These stories addressed the histories of natural resources and the economic and cultural forces behind their extraction.[4] I supplemented them with other big-picture works such as Jared Diamond's *Guns, Germs, and Steel: The Fates of Human Societies* (1997) and J. R. McNeill and William H. McNeill's *The Human Web: A Bird's-eye View of World History* (2003). Since then, big-picture thinking has seen astonishing successes, such as Yuval Noah Harari's *Sapiens: A Brief History of Humankind* (2011).[5]

With this reading course complete, I turned to literature, looking for the literary equivalent to world history. Unfortunately, there wasn't much. I made my way through different encyclopedias and reference works, but with the exception of a few classic such as Auerbach's *Mimesis* (1946), which unfortunately was focused on Western literature only, there existed nothing of the kind undertaken by historians.[6]

It was in the course of looking for large-scale work in vain that I began to feel the shortcomings of our literary education and scholarship, with their deep roots in national traditions, their near-exclusive focus on narrow timescales, their suspicion of synthetic scholarship and of asking larger questions about their object of study. It didn't matter whether you were a formalist or materialist, whether you reveled in close reading or historical context, whether you wanted to decode the secret meaning of texts or stay on the surface, whether you were searching for structures or looking for moments when those structures broke down, there was one thing that everyone seemed to agree on: namely, that the scale of literary inquiry should be narrow, focused, and specific, that it was useless to zoom out.[7]

This was pretty much the configuration of the field as we encountered it when we were tasked to create a new edition of the *Norton Anthology of World Literature* in the mid-2000s. By we, I mean a group of editors that included Emily Wilson, Wiebke Denecke, Suzanne Akbari, Barbara Fuchs, Caroline Levine, and Pericles Lewis (I always think of my co-editors in chronological order, that is, the order of the time periods and volumes they were in charge of) as members of the core team. Together, and drawing on many other experts in different fields, we began to assemble the larger picture of literature that our discipline was so reluctant to offer. Creating this anthology was the most collaborative project I have ever undertaken, involving dozens of experts and consultation with hundreds of people. The list of acknowledgments is longer than any I have seen, and for good reason. Doing large-scale work in literature, as in any other area, requires collaboration on a scale that is rare in the humanities. In fact, I have come to believe that large-scale thinking is not widespread in the discipline of literature in part because our work habits and methods are much too individualistic to allow for the type of collaboration such projects require.[8]

At the same time, we editors received a crash course in publishing. Initially, we had thought that we would be in the exciting position of actually remaking the canon of world literature, at least to the extent that the *Norton Anthology* was contributing to it. And we knew that the Norton was the largest anthology of its kind, used in over a thousand colleges and high schools. For the first time in our lives as scholars, our work might have a measurable impact on how literature was taught.

Very quickly we learned that our fantasies of influence were largely misplaced. The very fact that our anthology was used by so many people meant that many stakeholders had a vested interest in the choices that shaped it. This fact was driven home to us during our very first editorial meeting, when our Norton editor, Pete Simon, presented us with a large stack of papers, the responses to a questionnaire he had sent to hundreds of teachers across the country. The point was clear: this was not *our* anthology; it was *theirs*. We were providing something that catered to the needs of teachers and students and had little to do with our own pet theories about world literature. I think we all remember it as a humbling experience: we were producing something with a particular purpose, and that purpose was to help teachers and students tackle as unwieldy a topic as world literature, collaborating with them on the kind of large-scale thinking shunned by most of the profession.

During the following months and years, we learned more about the anthology as an institution and genre. Even though some scholars worried that US anthologies were imposing a particular vision of literature on the rest of the world, we learned that these anthologies were actually designed exclusively for the North American market.[9] Instead of export products, world literature anthologies were import vehicles, trying to get American students to read foreign literature.

The geographic reach of the anthology within North America was even more surprising: I would have thought that it catered primarily to the cosmopolitan coasts of the United States. Instead, roughly half of our adopters were located in eleven southern states (which contained only 14 percent of the nation's population). Why?

Initially, these courses, and hence the anthologies catering to them, emphasized Western literature, but they gradually expanded their purview, driven by changes in migration, especially after 1965, when the

United States abolished immigration laws explicitly favoring immigrants from European countries, as well as by economic globalization. Gradually, anthologies changed as well, increasing the representation of non-Western literature.

Despite—or perhaps because of—the expansion of the canon of world literature as represented in anthologies, the 1980s and '90s experienced what is sometimes referred to as the "canon wars," debates over the representation of women, minority cultures, non-Western traditions, and other categories of representation.[10] As the canon wars intensified, many universities, especially coastal, elite institutions, moved away from mandatory general education programs based on great books and instead switched to distribution requirements. This was not the case in many southern universities, which held on to general education classes but slowly widened their scope from Western literature to world literature, with the result that these southern universities now have a much more robust commitment to world literature than coastal universities. I finally understood why so many of our adopters were located in the South and not, as I had expected, on the cosmopolitan coasts.

As far as the Norton anthology is concerned, this process of turning Western literature courses into world literature courses has recently been completed. Originally, we editors had been put in charge, not of a single anthology, but of a whole family of anthologies, which included the *Norton Anthology of World Literature* and the *Norton Anthology of Western Literature* as well as several shorter versions of both. Recently, we decided to discontinue the Western anthology, primarily because it lacked internal coherence. Routinely, we had included literature from Latin America and the Middle East as well as literature written in European colonial languages from other parts of the world, which meant that Western literature had come to be defined, essentially, as world literature minus East Asia. This definition didn't make a lot of sense, to put it mildly; there was also less and less demand for such an anthology, and we finally decided to merge Western literature with world literature.[11]

Based on what I learned from my colleagues and collaborators, I want to suggest that world literature anthologies can attune teachers and students to large-scale questions, including those related to the environment. And because world literature anthologies are typically used in large, general education courses, they can be particularly effective in introducing nonspecialist students to the literary dimension of climate change.

I have dwelled on world literature anthologies because of my own experience with them and should add that they are by no means the only vehicle for large-scale thinking about literature, nor necessarily the best one.[12] Other, alternative paths include new quantitative approaches to literature made possible by the emergence of searchable corpora of texts.[13]

Even though I don't engage in digital humanities myself, I have high hopes for this kind of approach because it will make available the kind of scale I found lacking in my own literary education.[14] Yet another attractive model of large-scale thinking has been proposed by Wai Chee Dimock, who has called for deep-time reading habits that focus on resonances across significant time periods.[15] What matters, to my mind, is less *how* but *whether* we arrive at large-scale thinking about literature and the environment so that we can add this type of attention to our literary tool kit by whatever means available.

Based on what I have learned from both ecocriticism and world literature, I want to sketch a protocol for environmental reading that draws on the insights of both fields.[16]

A READING PROTOCOL

1. When reading a work of literature, never forget that you are dealing with a medium that is complicit with, and therefore most likely defensive of, settled life and the resource extraction required to sustain it. Any hope of literature resisting power or resource extraction is likely to be disappointed, or in any case an exception rather than the rule, especially in literature produced before the twentieth century (i.e., most of literature).

2. Literature's complicity with resource extraction is captured most directly in the fact that most of it, even today, is printed on paper, which is usually made from trees (paper was originally a Chinese invention, then traveled to the Arab world, and reached Europe via Arab-occupied Spain). Always relate the material base of literature, from writing materials to methods of distribution and reception, to its environmental costs and implications. This includes electronic databases and modes of distribution.

3. Literature not only sides with settled life but also tends to suppress orality. All written literature therefore should be related to oral traditions and the complex processes and interplay between writing and orality. Forms of orality might enable storytelling that is less complicit with settled life and that might allow a new perspective on it. Orality is often found at the margins of colonial empires and of modern states, but it also runs through the deep history of world literature. Writing and orality need to be understood as a single, interrelated system.

4. Writing's various forms of complicity with resource extraction mean that we have to read texts against the grain. In particular, this means paying attention to how texts draw the line between city and country, civilization and barbarism, human and animal, urban life and wilderness, and what kinds of attitudes toward nonsettled life, if any, they convey.

5. Since the basis for settled life is intensive agriculture in one form or another, pay attention to the way this agricultural base is treated, often in the margins, of literary texts. We literary scholars need to become conversant in the history of agriculture and other forms of resource extraction, from ancient Mesopotamia to the postindustrial age.

6. Given that climate change is not confined to one country and culture but has roots deep in human history, don't settle for explanations confined to specific areas and time periods. Instead, practice a mode of analysis at the scale of world literature, one that zooms in but also zooms out, relating specific case studies to larger questions of human behavior, inviting a broader, comparative perspective.

7. Neither the canons of world literature nor world literature anthologies are neutral tools. Much like literature itself, they are complicit with the resource-extracting way of life that has accelerated in the last two hundred years. But this complicity is not a reason to abandon them. On the contrary, it is what makes them so valuable for understanding how we arrived at this critical moment in human history.

CHAPTER FIVE

STORIES FOR THE FUTURE

THE REALIZATION THAT HUMANS are responsible for the sixth mass extinction—that we are the new meteorite—is forcing us to consider not only the stories of the past four thousand years but also what stories we should tell in the future.[1] What matters now, in other words, is not just interpreting world literature in new ways, but also changing it. This is, then, the moment for me to expand what has so far been mostly a two-way conversation between ecocriticism and world literature to include those producing new stories, whether fiction or nonfiction, and that means creative writers of all kinds. What does literary study have to say to current and future creative writers, both of fiction and nonfiction as well as to poets and dramatists, and to their interest in the environment?

In the many conversations I have had with writers and journalists as well as policymakers about the shaping power of stories, they have asked me questions such as: What do you, literary critics, know about the effects of stories on readers? What do you know about different types of stories? Which stories should we tell, and which ones avoid? It has been embarrassingly difficult to answer their questions with any degree of confidence. More than once have I found myself in a position of awkward equivocation.

In this situation, I have tended to default to what seemed like a safe bet: railing against Hollywood disaster movies. Surely, their apocalyptic endings seem to do nothing but induce paralysis and complacency, not targeted action. But this hypothesis, like so much in literary study, has not been tested. It is here that quantitative methods would be especially helpful, a wake-up call for the profession to deliver empirically tested knowledge about the effects of particular kinds of stories on readers.[2]

Fortunately, we now have, for the first time, tools that could be used for empirical information about the effects of stories—for example, with the user data available through storytelling websites such as Wattpad, a fan fiction company that possesses fascinating information about storytelling and reading that scholars of literature could use. The same, of course, is true of Amazon and other providers of e-readers and e-books. Fortunately, literary study has begun to make more room for this kind of empirical work.

In order to draw our new stories from the broadest possible base, what types of stories are out there that might be used or repurposed? Producing typologies of stories has been a strength of literary criticism. By some account, it is what scholars have been doing since Aristotle outlined the rules of tragedy in his *Poetics*. The only difficulty here is that there is little consensus, but this is as it should be. One might do worse, perhaps, than start with the most telegenic of schemes, one proposed by Kurt Vonnegut in a widely shared video (just google it, and you'll find it right away), in which he deadpans his way through three story types:

1. A protagonist of above-average happiness experiences ill fortune and falls into trouble. But things don't stay that way, and through grit and with some help from others, former happiness is restored. (Vonnegut called it "man in hole," adding that it doesn't have to be a man and it doesn't have to be a hole.) The graph begins moderately high, then drops down only to rise again significantly above the point of departure.

2. This story introduces an average protagonist who experiences an episode of good fortune only to lose it all, sinking deep. But then prospects brighten, and happiness is restored. (Vonnegut calls it "boy gets girl," adding that it doesn't have to be a boy and a girl.)

3. The third story type is the most well known. Vonnegut starts unusually low, with a little girl (this time he doesn't say that it doesn't have to be a girl) who has lost everything, before edging up when,

with the help of the fairy, this girl whom we know as Cinderella dresses up, goes to a ball, and dances with the prince. But this rise from bottom to top doesn't last; Cinderella is plunged back down, and all seems lost only for her fortunes to rise again, leading to her marriage to the prince.

Vonnegut's is just one of many attempts to map story types. Scholars, often with a structuralist bent, have singled out stories of rebirth and of overcoming monsters, of journey and return, of letting genies out of bottles and of revenge, stories of metamorphosis and of fools who triumph. They have classified stories according to genres and modes, from tragedy, comedy, and satire to romance and revolt. Individual story lines and story types can be further subdivided into their

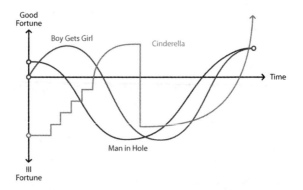

FIGURE 4. Chart showing three story types as described by Kurt Vonnegut in a lecture in 1985.

component parts, as was so powerfully demonstrated by Vladimir Propp, who identified thirty-one components at work in fairy tales.[3] Should we feel overwhelmed by this growing number of classifications, we can always turn to Joseph Campbell's reduction of all stories to a single one: *The Hero with a Thousand Faces.*[4]

As varied as these and many other schemes may be, there is plenty of material to work with for those turning to literary study to seek information about story types and plots. This knowledge, accumulated in different traditions of literary study over centuries and even millennia, is equally strong in non-Western criticism, including China, where one may begin with the "Great Preface" to the *Classic of Songs* (attributed, falsely, to Confucius), or the doctrine of rasas in South Asia, articulated by Bharata Muni in *Natya-shastra.* Literary criticism has yet to undergo the process of expansion that world literature anthologies began in the 1950s. Perhaps there should be a truly global anthology of literary criticism. Above all, this accumulated knowledge should be made available more widely and more readily for all those engaged in individual and collective acts of storytelling about the environment.

While literary study can contribute its deep knowledge about genre and plot types, there is one particular category of storytelling that is crucial for our purposes: agency. All stories need to figure out how to get from A to B, what drives them forward, whether it be divine intervention, individual agency, the aggregate of chance and circumstance, or some other driving force. The matter of agency is particularly important when it comes to a problem such as human-made climate change.

A vast number of stories focus on individual protagonists, on heroes with a thousand faces. To be sure, agency is usually more distributed, with other subagents helping along the way or hindering the path of the protagonist, and all kinds of other external circumstances playing their roles as well. But a protagonist is always a kind of concentration of agency, the ability to act on the world. In some cases, a story focused on an individual is understood to have wider implications for an entire society, as is the case with epic literature. Here, individual agents, such as Gilgamesh and Enkidu, are often located somewhere between gods and ordinary humans, enacting dramas of collective, even cosmic importance, or else they are kings whose actions radiate out over an entire nation.

For our changing planet, two questions of agency have been paramount: who is to blame, and who suffers the most. An increasing (and, to my mind, just) consensus holds that special blame should be assigned to early industrialized nations that have spent more time emitting CO_2 than more recently industrialized ones. Some might object that this is an instance of retroactive justice since early industrialized countries emitted CO_2 unwittingly, at least until the scientific consensus about human-made climate change started to coalesce around forty years ago. Does this mean it would be better to start counting forty years ago? I don't think so, since these same industrial power-houses of the nineteenth and early twentieth centuries accumulated wealth that now puts them in a position to mitigate and take responsibility for their unwitting and, more recently, their witting actions.

Sometimes this question of laying blame on entire nations is too crude since populations profited un-evenly from early as well as from current emissions. A more targeted approach might focus on oil companies, especially those that continue to explore new reserves, reserves they know need to stay in the ground. Those companies, of course, are also often responsible for deliberately sowing confusion and doubt about cli-mate science.[5]

Because of the human predilection for storytelling, we tend to personalize agents, concentrating agency in individuals or figures. Among the figures populat-ing our discourse on climate change are the hippie who unplugs from the grid, living a life of subsistence virtue (often depending on agriculture, though prac-ticed on a smaller scale); the oil lobbyist who seeks to obfuscate human responsibility for climate change; the Prius-driving recycler who flies a lot; the climate scientist whose warnings are ignored by the general population; the late-capitalist consumer who does not care about the environmental cost of commodities. Depending on where you stand, these figures will be exemplars of vice or virtue.

These heroes and villains are joined by a third, equally crucial figure: the victim. The tendency to focus on victims sometimes goes by the name of *climate justice*, the focus on groups most affected by climate change, from inhabitants of low-lying island nations to the most vulnerable groups within more powerful nations, those who have the least resources for withstanding the effects of climate change.

Here, we can look back at a long history of literary victims, stories about the weak and vulnerable. That history undeniably shows that victim stories are often immensely powerful. They include the passion of Christ as recounted in the gospels, perhaps one of the most influential stories of victimhood in world literature, as well as the story of Sunjata, who grows up handicapped and must overcome this physical impediment before becoming the ruler of his land. Modern stories have introduced a whole array of new outcasts, beginning with Don Quixote, and turned them into unlikely heroes (or antiheroes).

Heroes, villains, and victims: as with all figures of the environmental imagination, the reliance on these figures is not inherently good or bad; they serve different purposes at different times. My point is simply to call attention to the power these figures hold over environmental discourse to open them up to critical scrutiny where that is warranted. (For example, victim stories tend to remove agency from victims despite the fact that victimized communities have tended to exhibit enormous acts of resilience in the face of climate disaster. Conversely, stories focused on villains bundle all agency in the villain and disregard the extent to which villains respond to external pressures and systems.)

Another important and potentially useful figure for climate discourse is the settler, especially in societies founded by what Mahmood Mamdani has described as settler colonialism.[6] One might relate this figure of the settler to a whole series of settlement movements, celebrated throughout world literature, beginning with the *Epic of Gilgamesh*. The move toward settlement happened in different parts of the world in different ways, but it has drawn greater and greater swaths of humanity into its vortex. In its broadest definition, the settler is the kind of animal almost all humans have evolved into through a set of collective choices made by their ancestors. Not all settlers are the same, just as not all practices of intensive agriculture are the same, but it is worth noting that in today's world, very few people live outside the regime of either, which means that almost all humans are the descendants of Enkidu, having been brought into agricultural life.

Focusing on the figure of the settler in turn raises the question of who does not fall within that category: the nomad. There has been a war going on between the settler and the nomad ever since the introduction of agriculture, settlements, and cities. Step by step, larger swaths of humans have been brought into the settled life, voluntarily or involuntarily, but this process has never been complete. There still exist small numbers of nomadic peoples living outside settled society.[7] Perhaps "outside" isn't the right word, since the settler principle has encroached upon most corners of the world. Today, nomadism happens within, in the interstices of, the settled world.[8]

Different from, but related to, both the settler and the nomad is the refugee, a figure defined by being displaced from settlement and seeking shelter elsewhere. A good number of today's political refugees, from North Africa to Latin America, are in fact climate refugees, either directly or indirectly so, and the number of such refugees is predicted to increase steeply in the coming decades. Settled societies will be transformed—unsettled—by the arrival of climate refugees, with profound consequences.

Each of these figures, from the hero, the villain, and the victim to the settler, the nomad, and the refugee, has shaped the discourse on climate change. If we want to question existing storytelling and open up spaces for new stories to emerge, we need to ask whether this particular array of figures is the right one, sufficient for the task at hand. Should new figures be added? Should existing ones be deployed differently? Questions upon questions, which I can't answer, but at least I want to raise them.

There is another aspect to the human tendency toward personalization: the collective. For one thing is certain: climate change is produced not individually but collectively. There is no living and breathing human being that does not contribute, in however small a portion, to human-made climate change. In the last analysis, climate change is a matter of humans as a species, as a collective agent. And just as climate change is produced collectively, it will have to be solved collectively, no matter how important it is for individuals and institutions to do their part depending on guilt and suffering, ability, willingness, and necessity. What this means is that we need stories with collective agents.

I can think of one relatively recent model that might help here, a work of world literature that I have already discussed briefly in another context and that happens to have introduced a new collective agent: *The Communist Manifesto*. One feature that distinguishes this text from many of its rivals is that it tells a grand story of human society, a large-scale history as seen through the lens of class struggle. The *Manifesto* predicts its revolutionary future based on and as a culmination of this grand history. The historical forces behind this history, the *Manifesto* explains, conspire to create a new kind of collective agent.

Previously, Marx and Engels had encountered a discourse that revolved around two figures: the greedy capitalist, always depicted with a cigar in his (mostly male) mouth; and the victimized industrial workers. Marx and Engels acknowledged the truth of these two figures but also their limitations. They took the first, the capitalist, and depersonalized it, turning the villain into a structure (much as structural racism is shifting the discourse from individual attitudes to social structures and institutions). And they took the second, the mass of exploited victims, and turned them into a new and active agent: the proletariat.

The proletariat is not simply a group of victims who share the same predicament, such as being exploited by industrialization. Rather, the proletariat is the result of a historical process that has led to what we could call globalization—the relevant passage in the *Manifesto* ends with the invocation of *world literature*—which in turn has given rise to a new agent. While being the product of a historical process, this new agent needs to be distilled and articulated, it needs to be made manifest, and this is precisely the job of the *Manifesto*. In making the proletariat manifest, the *Manifesto* tells the story of the creation of a new agent and thereby brings this new agent into being (in the sense of making it visible *as* a new agent).

Interestingly, while thinking about how to launch their new agent, Marx and Engels begin to see the *Manifesto* as itself belonging to world literature: "Communists of various nationalities have assembled in London and sketched the following manifesto, to be published in the English, French, German, Italian, Flemish and Danish languages." The *Manifesto*'s original language—German—is listed simply as one among many. The authors envision, or rather fantasize, that their text will be published in many languages simultaneously.

Initially, it remained exactly that: a fantasy. There was almost no response when the *Manifesto* was published in London in 1848, and very few translations followed, especially over the next twenty years, a period in which the revolutionary fervor of 1848 gave way to a period of reaction.

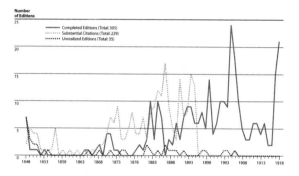

FIGURE 5. Unrealized editions, substantial citations, and realized editions of the *Communist Manifesto* between 1848 and 1918.

While the number of editions and translations was disappointing, the *Manifesto*'s status as world literature could already be perceived by the fact that many translations and editions were produced in exile, often because of censorship.[9] It was only with the Paris Commune and the Russian Revolution that the *Manifesto* became a text of global significance, finally fulfilling its goal of introducing a new agent into world history.

FIGURE 6. (*Top*) Places and languages of publication of the *Communist Manifesto* between 1848 and 1869.

	German	English	Russian	Swedish
1848	London (4)			Stockholm
1849	Kassel			
1850	London-Hamburg	London		
1851	New York			
1853	Berlin			
1864	London			
1866	London-Berlin			
1868	Vienna			
1869		London	Geneva	

FIGURE 7. (*Right*) Places and languages of publication of the *Communist Manifesto* between 1871 and 1892.

	German	English	Russian	Swedish	French	Spanish	Czech	Polish	Danish	Italian	Bulgarian	Serbo-Croatian	Dutch	Yiddish	Rumanian
1871	Chicago	New York										Pancevo (Serbia) [2]			
1872	Leipzig (2)				New York	Madrid									
1873	Berlin					Lisbon									
1874	Vienna Chicago Leipzig														
1879					Lugano										
1880	London				Paris										
1881	London														
1882			Moscow Geneva				New York								
1883	Chicago Zürich	New York (2)	St. Petersb. (3) Krakow Moscow					Geneva							
1884	Zürich				Paris				Copenhagen						
1885			St. Petersburg Moscow Kazan		Paris Reems Montluçon Roubaix Roanne				Copenhagen						
1886		London	St. Petersburg	Stockholm	Paris	Madrid (2)			Christiania (Oslo)						
1888		London (2)													
1889						Mexico			Copenhagen	Cremona					
1890	New York	New York (2)	Moscow		Paris									London	
1891	Berlin									Milan	Ruse				
1892	Bern									Milan			Amsterdam Hague		Iasi (2)

Can we learn something from this history for environmental change? The first lesson is how difficult it is to envision a new, collective agent. In order to accomplish this goal, Marx and Engels had to invent not only a new approach to history but also an entirely new genre in which to tell it: the genre of the manifesto. Is it time for a new manifesto for environmental thinking and reading and living?

I have been struck by the extent to which recent social movements, from Occupy Wall Street to Black Lives Matter, have shied away from the manifesto as a genre. One reason, perhaps, is the discrediting of the specific story told in this text and therefore the particular agent, the industrial proletariat, as envisioned by the two authors. But the deeper reason for widespread skepticism with regard to the manifesto lies elsewhere, I believe, and has to do with the *Manifesto*'s first-person plural. The "we" of the manifesto sounds presumptuous, especially to ears that have become so attuned to the dangers of universalizing particular experiences and of speaking for others. The default, today, is to encourage everybody to speak only for themselves, or for a narrowly defined group.

Here, it may be instructive to see how exactly the two authors came to use the "we." In the *Manifesto*, Marx and Engels don't speak for themselves at all; by "we," they don't mean "Marx and Engels." Rather, they speak for an entity, the institution that hired them: the Communist League. In fact, Marx and Engels didn't originally appear as authors of the published text. They didn't even sign it. They didn't speak for themselves at all. They simply produced a text for the Communist League to allow this league to articulate its own principles and goals.

The Communist League was not a powerful institution. On the contrary, it was a weak, small assortment of mostly German-speaking artisans living in London. In assuming the "we" of the manifesto, with its grand historical vision and the introduction of a new historical agent, the league was nothing if not presumptuous. Speaking from a position of obscurity and powerlessness, it assumed the voice of collective power.

Can literary scholars hoping to contribute to the knowledge of climate change distributed across our field learn something from this presumptuous audacity? I believe so. It is that speaking as a "we" doesn't have to mean "I speak for you"; it can mean that an obscure and powerless association of people can commission two of its members (or more, or fewer) to articulate a new historical agent. Something like this is possible. At least, it has happened before.

How could anyone define the collective agent that would rise up to solve climate change? Such an act would require figuring out how to tell the story of that agent, what constellation of historical forces might produce it. Finally, it would mean deciding how best to make that agent visible, what kind of manifesto or other genre would bring it to the forefront of our understanding.[10]

Recently, one particular environmental disaster has emerged that has forced humans all over the world to reckon with itself as a species: Covid-19. The virus causing this illness—like other viruses—is the result of the settled agricultural lifestyle that brought humans and animals into close proximity, creating the conditions for the virus to jump from animals to humans. Its deadly effects target humans as a species since the virus has found humans, due to their very abundance, as its most effective vehicle for replicating itself. In the process, Covid-19 is changing humans on the level of a species in the sense that our bodies will change in the coming years.

This kind of species thinking is very different from the abstract (and yet, in an unacknowledged manner, culturally specific) notion of humans propagated by Renaissance humanists or eighteenth-century universalist philosophers. Acknowledging the "species" dimension in the sense of a differentiated collectivity doesn't prevent us from seeing vast differences in how nations and groups within nations have been affected by this virus. If anything, the virus has revealed these differences all the more starkly.

I am writing these lines in April 2020, in the middle of what is likely to be only the first peak. But even at this point in time, two things are clear. The pressure and pain brought by this virus has resulted in heightened nationalisms, with different countries blaming one another or otherwise competing. At the same time, it has become evident that the virus does not respect national boundaries and is forcing us to reckon with our existence as a species. The effects of the virus on the environmental movement are as yet uncertain. But I believe the virus has forced us into recognizing the differentiated collectivity that will be crucial for addressing other aspects of climate change. My hope is that such a collectivity will allow for the recognition of specific groups within species thinking without playing off particular groups against each other or against the species.[11]

From an environmental perspective, humans aren't the only species that should feature in climate narratives. In fact, it is striking that the newer environmental literature focuses on other species and our relation to them. Richard Powers' *Overstory* is a recent and justly noted work of literature about trees; there are excellent narrative experiments in the species being of butterflies and mushrooms.[12] These works don't isolate the species they study but turn them into agents in an ecosystem that includes humans. (My thinking about species is also influenced by another manifesto, Donna J. Haraway's *The Companion Species Manifesto.*)[13]

But even if literary scholars, working with scientists and environmental activists, could produce an account of collective agency, who would write such a new narrative? Perhaps more so than in the nineteenth century, there would need to be a collective process of involvement, perhaps even a collective act of articulation. Mere delegation, as in the case of Marx and Engels, would probably not be enough.

There is a type of world literature that can perhaps be a guide to a collective storytelling process: medieval story collections such as the *Panchatantra* or the *Arabian Nights*. The appeal of aggregating stories is to get away from another figure that has held a lot of thinking about literature in its thrall: the individual author. For most of literary history—to return one last time to the big-picture history of writing—literature was produced by people other than authors. Instead, it was produced by scribes, editors, and collectors who inherited texts and produced new ones according to very different principles from those prevailing among modern authors. For one thing, originality was not a prized value for much of this history. Much more important was the task of continuing a tradition and imitating cultural objects from the past while perhaps introducing subtle changes or adapting the past to present needs under the guise of continuity. Sometimes, such changes happened haphazardly, through scribal errors or else through deliberate or involuntary acts of misreading.

Such collective values arising from literary works were slowly pushed to the side with the rise of modern authors, who concocted new, original stories, laid claim to owning those stories, and sold them in the marketplace. This type of author predated the rise of the printing press but became dominant with the mechanization of the printing press in northern Europe and the industrial mass production of literature.

It so happens that we live in an age when collecting, aggregating, and compiling have become newly central again, after centuries when individual authors claimed center stage. Curating has become an activity not just for a few highly placed museum employees but something available to many. At the same time, the term's meaning has expanded and now includes any activity that involves picking and choosing, compiling and collecting, the creation of playlists and photo albums. Can this curatorial frenzy be trained on the task of collecting stories that might bring about a better future?

There are interesting modern storytelling aggregators, including storytelling websites, that might give hints as to more collective modes of storytelling. Needless to say, this storytelling activity would have to come from all over the world. But who would host such a storytelling website or festival? And how would such a collection of stories be framed, perhaps in the manner of the frame-tale narratives of old? As important as I find it to raise these questions, I am myself at a loss for answers and hope that others will supply what I cannot.

The uncertainty about future stories is compounded by the rise of a new era of world literature. Never before has the canon of world literature been more easily available than today. At the same time, the material conditions of literature are changing fast, thanks to new media of reproduction and dissemination. How will these transformations change the stories we read and the ones that are yet unwritten?

The new age of abundance in which ever more stories are vying for attention is relatively unprecedented. For most of its history, literary texts had to struggle for survival because considerable resources had to be spent on preserving and transcribing them from one generation to the next, while many texts were lost through library fires (such as the library of Nineveh, which housed the *Epic of Gilgamesh*) and other acts of willful or accidental destruction. An interruption in transmission for even a few generations would mean almost certain loss. Much rarer were moments when lost texts could be recovered after a significant hiatus (as was the case with the *Epic of Gilgamesh*).

Texts survived not only through their material existence but also through their significance, because they were seen as precious and important, justifying the costly education of scribes and commentators, who in turn communicated the importance of these texts to those controlling resources. These economic pressures lessened as the cost of storage dropped and the production and reproduction of literature became cheaper. Initially, this drop in costs was brought about by the invention of paper and of print in China, creating a virtuous cycle of rising literacy rates that increased the demand for literature, the production of which in turn made literacy rates rise even more.[14]

Today we are living through yet another change in the underlying technologies of literature in that the cost of storage, for the first time in human history, is dropping toward zero (though not the environmental cost; even today, literature remains complicit with our resource-extracting mode of life). This means that the evolving canon of literature will be defined much less by the accidents of survival, although there are still significant dangers in relying on electronic storage. The obsolescence of electronic formats and media is an underappreciated problem, and websites need to be constantly tended and updated.

Despite these caveats, it is clear that we are living in an age of abundance, an age when a large amount of cultural objects from the past and the present are available to us thanks to cheap storage and distribution. This age places different pressures on selection in the form of filters and search mechanisms, but also in the form of education. Education means communicating significance—and nothing is more significant today than environmental change. Teaching world literature with reference to climate change is also a way of making the canon of literature newly relevant to the next generation. What we don't use, we lose, whether to the ravages of time or to the neglected parts of the internet that will become inaccessible in less than a generation.

While literature can help us understand our current environmental crisis, the reverse is thus also true: the climate crisis brings into focus the significance of literature. The importance of literature for our changing planet coincides fatefully with the decline of the humanities. The tried-and-true methods seem to be failing, leading to widespread fears of irrelevance. Everyone has their pet theories about what went wrong and who is to blame. I myself no longer feel I know what it is that we should do, only that we can't continue as we have. We have tried that approach, and it doesn't work. Somehow, we must find new ways to win over students and their parents, climate scientists and scholars in other disciplines, university administrators, activists working in NGOs and thinktanks, as well as the general public. The climate crisis is a chance for us to get our act together. By trying to help save the planet, the humanities might manage to save themselves.

But the fate of the humanities, large as it looms to those connected with them, pales in comparison to the fate of the humans. What shall become of this resource-extracting storyteller? Will we be willing to listen to tales with harsh lessons and demanding conclusions? It has happened before. Humans have shown that they don't simply produce literature to feel good about themselves but also to face hard choices and to engage in collective action. After all, the ability to coordinate our minds through language was what first jump-started the accelerated cultural development that set us apart from the rest of life on earth. Now the same communicative tools must come to our aid in acts of collective storytelling. Is it time for the storytellers of the world to unite?[15]

ACKNOWLEDGMENTS

THIS BOOK EMERGED FROM a new lecture series jointly sponsored by Oxford University and Princeton University Press, so my first thanks go to Philip Bullock, of the Oxford Humanities Center (TORCH), and Ben Tate, of Princeton University Press, who masterminded the visit brilliantly. I was extremely fortunate to spend two weeks lodged in the modernist environs of Wolfson College, founded by Isaiah Berlin and more recently headed by Hermione Lee, as the guest of Julie Curtis. During my time at Oxford, I profited from conversations with some old friends and many new ones, including Marta Arnaldi, Stefano-Maria Evangelista, Laura Marcus, Peter McDonald, Ben Morgan, Ankhi Mukherjee, Karen O'Brian, Ritchie Robertson, Ralph Schroeder, Kirsten Shepherd-Barr, and Bart van Es (and, during a secret side trip to Cambridge, with Claire Foster, Efe Khayyat, Robert Tombs, and Esther-Miriam Wagner). The two weeks were among the most enjoyable academic experiences I can remember.

There had been earlier occasions for me to try out and shape some of the material that made it into these lectures, including during a wonderful two-week stay at Queen Mary University of London, hosted by Kiera Vaclavik and Galin Thianov, during which time I was fortunate to exchange thoughts with Edward Hughes, Angus Nicholls, and Isabelle Parkinson, especially about anthologies as a genre. Additionally, I enjoyed other occasions for exchange during two weeks spent at Tsinghua University, hosted by Yan Haiping, and during a visit to the University of Columbia, Missouri, hosted by Noah Herringman.

My foray into world literature was originally facilitated by my work on the *Norton Anthology of World Literature*, as mentioned in the lectures, so I also wish to thank Pete Simon, my Norton editor, as well as my co-editors Suzanne Akbari, Wiebke Denecke, Barbara Fuchs, Caroline Levine, Pericles Lewis, and Emily Wilson along with the many teachers and students of world literature I have interacted with over the years.

There are a few more people to thank, including the three anonymous readers who reviewed the written text; Ellen Foos, who shepherded the manuscript through production; Daniel Simon, who copyedited the manuscript; Lisa Randall, who helped me understand cosmology; and, as always, Amanda Claybaugh, whose infallible sense of structure made me rethink the narrative, and whose love and companionship sustain everything I do.

Finally, I want to acknowledge two decades' worth of conversation about climate change with Ursula

Heise and an equal number of conversations about world literature with David Damrosch, which is why this book is dedicated to these two colleagues and friends.

ILLUSTRATION CREDITS

FIGURE 1. Alexander von Humboldt and A. G. Bonpland, "Geographie der Pflanzen in den Tropen-Ländern," in Alexander von Humboldt, *Ideen zu einer Geographie der Pflanzen* (Tübingen: Leibniz Institut für Länderkunde, 1807), map 1. Creative Commons CC0 1.0 Universal Public Domain Dedication. Source: Wikimedia.

FIGURE 2. Nineteenth-century photograph of Crompton, near Manchester, England. Source: Wikimedia.

FIGURE 3. Rococo Hall of Duchess Anna Amalia Library, Weimar. Creative Commons CC0 1.0 Universal Public Domain Dedication. Source: Wikimedia.

FIGURE 4. Wave chart illustrating Kurt Vonnegut's three story types. Courtesy: Kailey E. Bennett.

FIGURE 5. Wave chart showing unrealized editions, substantial citations, and realized editions of the *Communist Manifesto* between 1848 and 1918. Source: Martin Puchner, *Poetry of the Revolution: Marx, Manifestos, and the Avant-Gardes* (Princeton: Princeton University Press, 2006), 39.

FIGURE 6. Chart showing the places and languages of publication of *The Communist Manifesto* between 1848 and 1869. Source: Puchner, *Poetry of the Revolution*, 64.

FIGURE 7. Chart showing the places and languages of publication of *The Communist Manifesto* between 1871 and 1892. Source: Puchner, *Poetry of the Revolution*, 65.

PREAMBLE.
LITERATURE FOR A CHANGING PLANET

1. An alternative hypothesis, promoted by my colleague Lisa Randall, holds that the projectile was a comet, which would have made its journey even longer. It would have likely originated in the Oort cloud, in the outermost reaches of the solar system, 2,000 AU from earth (1 AU is 93 million miles). This would have also made it about three times as fast as the asteroid, about 120,000mph as opposed to "only" 40,000mph. Lisa Randall, *Dark Matter and the Dinosaurs: The Astounding Interconnectedness of the Universe* (New York: Ecco, 2015), 271ff.

2. Michael Pollan, *The Omnivore's Dilemma: A Natural History of Four Meals* (New York: Penguin, 2006).

3. This is partly an argument in favor of using literary study for nonliterary ends. Some readers may wonder how that connects to the debate started by Rita Felski about the uses of literature—and literary criticism. See Rita Felski, *Uses of Literature* (Oxford: Blackwell, 2008), and *The Limits of Critique* (Chicago: University of Chicago Press, 2015). For a recent discussion of this approach, also see the podcast on fictional empathy with Rita Felski and Namwali Serpell in conversation with John Plotz: *Recall This Book*, episode 18, https://recallthisbook.org/2019/11/14/18-fictional-empathy-rita-felski-and-namwali-serpell-with-jp. While I am sympathetic to Felski's sense of the limitations of literary criticism, the process of writing these

lectures has reminded me of the importance of critique. I have come to believe that using literary study for the purposes of mitigating climate change, as I am arguing here, does require a particular form of critique. Such a critique would incorporate many of Felski's points, however.

4. Lawrence Buell, *Writing for an Endangered World: Literature, Culture, and Environment in the U.S. and Beyond* (Cambridge: Belknap Press, 2001).

5. Rob Nixon, *Slow Violence and the Environmentalism of the Poor* (Cambridge, Mass.: Harvard University Press, 2013). Stephanie LeMenager, *Living Oil: Petroleum Culture in the American Century* (Oxford: Oxford University Press, 2014).

6. On MFA programs, see Mark McGurl, *The Program Era: Postwar Fiction and the Rise of Creative Writing* (Cambridge, Mass.: Harvard University Press, 2009). As always, there are significant exceptions (i.e., teachers in MFA programs with an interest in climate change). One of them is Rob Nixon, who is both a scholar of environmental violence and currently teaches creative nonfiction writing at Princeton. Rob Nixon, *Slow Violence and the Environmentalism of the Poor* (Cambridge, Mass.: Harvard University Press, 2013).

7. A notable exception is Ursula Heise, with her books *Sense of Place and Sense of Planet: The Environmental Imagination of the Global* (Oxford: Oxford University Press, 2008), *Nach der Natur: Das Artensterben und die moderne Kultur* (Frankfurt am Main: Suhrkamp, 2010), and *Imagining Extinction: The Cultural Meanings of Endangered Species* (Chicago: University of Chicago Press, 2016). Wai Chee Dimock's excellent new book, *Weak Planet: Literature and Assisted Survival* (Chicago: Chicago University Press, 2020), was published too late to be fully absorbed into these lectures. I found the book extremely *simpático* with what I was trying to do here.

8. Ursula Heise writes: "Most of the texts that ecocritics have studied since the emergence of their field in the early 1990s have achieved distinction in particular national traditions of nature

writing—Britain, Germany, or the United States—without attaining the international circulation that would integrate them into the canon of world literature." "World Literature and the Environment," in *The Routledge Companion to World Literature*, edited by Theo D'haen, David Damrosch, and Djelal Kadir (London: Routledge, 2012): 404–412, 404.

9. What I want to accomplish with these ruminations, then, is to convince readers of world literature that they can learn from ecocriticism just as ecocriticism may find in world literature an expanded field of inquiry, while fiction and nonfiction writers might be able to learn more fully from both. Another way of putting this is to say that the three groups of people I care much about, namely ecocritics, teachers of world literature (who teach many of the general education courses taken by nonspecialists), and MFA students, don't talk as much to one another as they might. What I hope to do is to facilitate a three-way conversation, with my role not so much that of an expert—I am not an expert in ecocriticism; no one can be an expert in world literature; and I am not teaching in an MFA program—but as a host.

CHAPTER ONE.
READING IN A WARMING WORLD

1. Sir Austen Henry Layard, *Nineveh and Its Remains, in Two Volumes* (London: John Murray, 1849), 1:70.

2. For an account of the discovery and decipherment of cuneiform script, read the excellent book by David Damrosch, *The Buried Book: The Loss and Rediscovery of the Great Epic of Gilgamesh* (New York: Henry Holt, 2006).

3. One of the few scholars interested in environmental literature to have recognized the importance of the *Epic of Gilgamesh* is Roy Scranton in his unusual book *Learning to Die in the Anthropocene: Reflections on the End of a Civilization* (San Francisco: City Lights, 2015).

4. Robert Alter, Genesis 6, in *The Norton Anthology of World Literature*, 4th ed., volume A (New York: Norton, 2018), 157ff.

5. *The Epic of Gilgamesh*, translated by Benjamin R. Foster (New York: Norton, 2001), XI, 173, 186.

6. *Gilgamesh*, XI, 187.

7. *Gilgamesh*, XI, 191–196.

8. *Gilgamesh*, I, 11–24.

9. James C. Scott, *Against the Grain: A Deep History of the Earliest States* (New Haven: Yale University Press, 2017).

10. For a discussion of Scott's *Against the Grain*, see my review essay "Down with the Scribes?" *Public Books*, April 16, 2018, https://www.publicbooks.org/down-with-the-scribes (retrieved October 11, 2020). I should add that I have since come around to Scott's point much more than I did when I first read and reviewed his book.

11. *Gilgamesh*, V, 57.

12. *Gilgamesh*, V, 108–109.

13. *Gilgamesh*, V, 111ff.

14. Jedediah Purdy, *This Land Is Our Land: The Struggle for a New Commonwealth* (Princeton: Princeton University Press, 2019).

15. Homer, *The Odyssey*, translated by Emily Wilson (New York: Norton, 2018), 9, 108–111.

16. *Odyssey*, 9, 111–115.

17. *Odyssey*, 9, 382–394.

18. *Odyssey*, 9, 219.

19. *Odyssey*, 9, 403ff.

20. My favorite translation of Virgil's *Georgics* is by Janet Lembke, who was a superb classicist and naturalist in equal measure. *Virgil's Georgics: A New Verse Translation* (New Haven: Yale University Press, 2005). I also want to credit Stephanie Bernhard for her reading of Virgil's *Georgics*, which is part of her excellent dissertation and book-in-progress. I also find myself very much in sympathy with her idea of studying "species stories," how we narrate our own history as a species, something I propose toward the end of this book.

21. Amitav Ghosh, *The Great Derangement: Climate Change and the Unthinkable* (London: Penguin, 2016).

22. As always, there are fascinating exceptions to this rule, like pre-eighteenth-century retreats into wild nature. My favorite is Kamo no Chōmei, *The Ten Foot Square Hut*, a short work of fiction from twelfth-century Japan that describes a Buddhist monk's retreat into a mountain hut.

CHAPTER TWO.
A REVOLUTION IN ACCOUNTING

1. There is one mention of writing in an interpolated tale narrated by Bellerophon in the *Iliad* (*Iliad* VI, 168–170). The episode demonstrates the treachery of writing: the messenger carries a message that asks the recipient to kill the messenger. Writing did not exist in the Bronze-age Greece of the Trojan War, but it is instructive that Homer introduces it here as a warning about the treachery of this new technology.

2. "Enmerkar and the Lord of Aratta," translated by Herman Vanstiphout, in *The Norton Anthology of World Literature*, 1074–1076.

3. For more details on the *Popol Vuh*, see Dennis Tedlock, *2000 Years of Mayan Literature,* with new translations and interpretations by the author (Berkeley: University of California Press, 2010), as well as my own chapter on this text in *The Written World: The Power of Stories to Shape People, History, and Civilization* (New York: Random House, 2017): 171–192.

4. *Popol Vuh: The Definitive Edition of the Mayan Book of the Dawn of Life and the Glories of Gods and Kings*, translated by Dennis Tedlock (New York: Touchstone, 1985), 68.

5. *Popol Vuh*, 69.

6. *Popol Vuh*, 73.

7. *Popol Vuh*, 146.

8. Jared Diamond, *Guns, Germs, and Steel: The Fates of Human Society* (New York: Norton, 1997).

9. Inga Clendinnen, *Ambivalent Conquests: Maya and Spaniard in Yucatan, 1517–1570*, 2nd ed. (Cambridge: Cambridge University Press, 2003), 17ff.

10. Friar Diego de Landa, *Yucatan Before and After the Conquest*, translated with notes by William Gates (New York: Dover, 1978), 82.

11. De Landa, *Yucatan Before and After the Conquest*, 12, 19.

12. Tedlock, *2000 Years of Mayan Literature*, 299.

13. *The Epic of Sunjata*, edited and translated by David C. Conrad, in *The Norton Anthology of World Literature*, 4th ed., volume C (New York: Norton, 2018): 12–58, 36.

14. David C. Conrad, "Islam in the Oral Traditions of Mali: Bilali and Surakata," *Journal of African History* 26, no. 1 (1985): 33–49.

15. See also my *The Written World: The Power of Stories to Shape People, History, and Civilization* (New York: Random House, 2017): 290–305.

16. See David C. Conrad, *Sunjata: A New Prose Version,* edited and translated with an introduction by David C. Conrad (Indianapolis: Hackett, 2016); and Robert C. Newton, *The Epic Cassette: Technology, Tradition, and Imagination in Contemporary Bamana Segu,* PhD diss., University of Wisconsin–Madison (Ann Arbor: UMI, 1997).

17. See Kyle Powys Whyte, "Our Ancestors' Dystopia Now: Indigenous Conversation and the Anthropocene," in *The Routledge Companion to the Environmental Humanities*, ed. Ursula Heise, Jon Christensen, and Michelle Niemann (New York: Routledge, 2016), 206–214; and Whyte, "Critical Investigations of Resilience: A Brief Introduction to the Indigenous Environmental Studies and Sciences," *Daedalus* 147 (2018): 136–147. See also Dan Wildcat, *Red Alert: Saving the Planet with Indigenous Knowledge* (Golden, Colo.: Fulcrum Press, 2009). For a history of Native American print culture, see Phillip H. Rund, *Removable Type: Histories of the Book in Indian Country, 1663–1880* (Chapel Hill: University of North Caroline Press, 2010).

18. Kathryn Schulz, "The Really Big One," *New Yorker*, July 20, 2015, https://www.newyorker.com/magazine/2015/07/20/the-really-big-one.

CHAPTER THREE.
THE TWO FACES OF WORLD LITERATURE

1. Martin Puchner, "Readers of the World, Unite!" *Aeon*, September 20, 2017, https://aeon.co/essays/world-literature-is-both-a-market-reality-and-a-global-ideal. Also see David Damrosch, *What Is World Literature?* (Princeton: Princeton University Press, 2003), 1ff.

2. Ralph Waldo Emerson, *Representative Men: Seven Lectures* (Boston: Phillips, Sampson, 1850).

3. This account is based on Eckermann's autobiography, in Johann Peter Eckermann, *Gespräche mit Goethe in den letzten Jahren seines Lebens* (Leipzig: Brockhaus, 1837), 1:1–34.

4. Eckermann, *Gespräche*, 1:322.

5. Translation has sometimes been used as an argument against world literature. This has always puzzled me. It seems to me that we have a simple choice: either we restrict our reading to texts to which we have access in the original, which for most people means reading in a single language (or perhaps two or three), or we embrace translation as a welcome, indeed almost miraculous expansion of what any human can read. Arguing against translation erects a barrier that often strikes me as a thinly disguised strategy for professors of comparative literature to keep the unwashed masses (i.e., those without many languages) out. It is also extremely unkind to hard-working and often underpaid translators. Finally, it disregards the incredibly dynamic process of translation. My collaboration on the *Norton Anthology* has allowed me to work with extremely gifted translators, most importantly Emily Wilson, the classics editor who translated the *Odyssey* for the anthology. This translation has

become a smashing success, and rightly so. It is also the first translation of the *Odyssey* into English undertaken by a woman. This was part of our strategy, as editors, to use and commission more translations by women in order to insert female voices into a period of world literature that allowed very few women to write. For further reading in this debate, see Caroline Levine, "For World Literature," *Public Books*, January 6, 2014, https://www.publicbooks.org/for-world-literature. I also recommend Emily Wilson, "Introduction," in *The Odyssey*, translated by Emily Wilson (New York: Norton, 2018): 1–80.

6. Johann Wolfgang von Goethe, *Italienische Reise*, in *Autobiographische Schriften III, Hamburger Ausgabe in 14 Bänden* (Munich: Verlag H. C. Beck, 1994), 11:252.

7. Goethe, *Reise*, 299.

8. Andrea Wulf, *The Invention of Nature: Alexander von Humboldt's New World* (New York: Knopf, 2015).

9. David Damrosch, *Comparing the Literatures: Literary Studies in a Global Age* (Princeton: Princeton University Press, 2020), 52ff.

10. Edward Said, *Orientalism* (New York: Pantheon Books, 1976).

11. Karl Marx and Friedrich Engels, *The Communist Manifesto and Other Writings*, with an introduction and notes by Martin Puchner (New York: Barnes and Noble, 2005), 10–11. The translation is based on Samuel Moore's but updated by me.

12. In this sense, Marx and Engels are very different from recent environmental writers such as Naomi Klein, who argue that the fundamental changes necessary for avoiding the worst effects of climate change cannot come from within capitalism. Naomi Klein, *The Shock Doctrine: The Rise of Disaster Capitalism* (New York: Knopf, 2007).

13. Melekh Ravitsh and Borekh Rivkin, "Reflections on World Literature," in David Damrosch, ed., *World Literature in Theory* (Chichester, West Sussex: Blackwell/Wiley, 2013): 71–84; Rabindranath Tagore, "World Literature," in David Damrosch, ed., *World Literature in Theory* (Chichester, West Sussex: Blackwell/Wiley, 2013): 47–57.

14. Zheng Zhenduo, "A View on the Unification of Literature," in David Damrosch, ed., *World Literature in Theory* (Chichester, West Sussex: Blackwell/Wiley, 2013): 58–67.

CHAPTER FOUR.
HOW TO ANTHOLOGIZE THE WORLD

1. For more on these two figures, see Emily Apter, *The Translation Zone: A New Comparative Literature* (Princeton: Princeton University Press, 2006).

2. An exception to this rule is a group at Queen Mary University of London that has studied—and taught—this genre for years, under the leadership of Kiera Vaclavik and Isabelle Parkinson. As I mention in my acknowledgments, some of the lectures on which this book is based were held at QMUL before I refined and rewrote them for the inaugural lecture series jointly hosted by Princeton University Press and Oxford University in November 2019. Another scholar from whom I have learned much about anthologies is Leah Price, in her *The Anthology and the Rise of the Novel: From Richardson to George Eliot* (Cambridge: Cambridge University Press, 2000).

3. Mark Kurlansky's seafood trilogy consists of *Cod: A Biography of the Fish that Changed the World* (New York: Penguin Books, 1998), *Big Oyster: History of the Half-Shell* (New York: Random House, 2006), and *Salt: A World History* (New York: Penguin Books, 2002). Jared Diamond, *Guns, Germs, and Steel: The Fates of Human Societies* (New York: Norton, 1997). J. R. McNeill and William H. McNeill, *The Human Web: A Bird's-eye View of World History* (New York: Norton, 2003). Another example of commodity history is Jonathan Morris's *Coffee: A Global History* (London: Reaktion Books, 2019), which details the costs of America's recent infatuation with coffee.

4. I am also indebted to Bruce Robbins and his reflections on commodity histories in his article "Commodity Histories," *PMLA* 120, no. 2 (March 2005): 454–463.

5. Yuval Noah Harari, *Sapiens: A Brief History of Humankind* (New York: Harper, 2015).

6. Erich Auerbach, *Mimesis: Dargestellte Wirklichkeit in der abendländischen Literatur* (Zurich: A. Francke Verlag, 2946).

7. This trend received additional support from widespread warnings against grand narratives, the idea that any attempt to tell a larger story was nothing but an illegitimate attempt to elevate a particular experience into a universal one, at the expense of everyone else. The view had some justification in that, historically, those in power tended to tell themselves stories about their own importance, universalizing their particular values and literatures. Declaring universals was often a thinly disguised play for dominance, usually backed up by racist or colonialist assumptions. It was much better, many concluded, to abandon grand stories and instead study how particular texts disrupted attempts at generalization.

   While the political suspicion of universalism makes sense, both then and now, the conclusion to dismiss all large-scale thinking along with it is itself an example of turning a particular historical observation—how universal claims have been used to disguise power—into a universal one: all large-scale perspectives are disguised power plays. This dismissal of all large-scale thinking, I believe, has inadvertently kept literary study boxed into its national literature departments with their focus on small-scale questions and more limited conclusions. And this organization of the field has in turn made it difficult to obtain the kind of large-scale optic that can be so useful for certain purposes, including tackling problems such as climate change that operate on very large timescales.

8. To put this another way: it is not my intention at all to dismiss focused, specialized work. On the contrary, anyone working on larger-scale questions, including myself, is extremely depen-

dent on specialized work. My only point is that we should not discourage large-scale thinking. We simply need both. Right now, the study of literature leans heavily, I am tempted to say almost exclusively, toward focused work, hence my intervention in favor of large-scale approaches. A book I much admire in this regard is Edward W. Said, *Orientalism* (New York: Pantheon, 1979), which simultaneously warns against empty universals and yet practices the kind of big-picture thinking I am looking for.

9. Sometimes, world literature anthologies produced by US publishers are falsely described as export products, imposing a US vision of world literature on the rest of the world. I generally sympathize with worries about the distortions in world literature created by the dominance of English, but in the case of world literature anthologies, this worry seems to me misguided. Far from export endeavors, world literature anthologies such as the Norton are import endeavors aiming to introduce more non-English literature into American classrooms. The same is true of the *Longman Anthology of World Literature* and the *Bedford Anthology of World Literature*. These anthologies are restricted to the North American market and cannot be sold abroad. One interesting reason is that there doesn't seem to exist a widespread practice of teaching general education world literature courses in other countries, though that is slowly changing. Where such practices exist, they don't use English-language translations.

10. An insightful take on this debate was articulated by John Guillory in "Canon, Syllabus, List: A Note on the Pedagogic Imaginary," *Transition*, no. 52 (1991): 36–54.

11. For a recent account of changes in world literature anthologies, see Markella Rutherford and Peggy Levitt, "Who's on the Syllabus? World Literature According to the US Pedagogical Canon," *Journal of World Literature* 5 (2020): 606–629.

12. I hope that anthologies might be used more often to address the literary dimension of climate change even though I and my collaborators, as well as other teams producing world literature

anthologies, have not foregrounded this environmental dimension in the organization of these anthologies, an omission I hope to change in the future. In other words, my exhortation to colleagues in world literature to engage more fully with ecocriticism is primarily directed at myself.

13. A prominent example is the work done at the Stanford Literary Lab. Originally created by Franco Moretti, the lab is now run by Mark Algee-Hewitt. Also see Franco Moretti, *Distant Reading* (London: Verso, 2013).

14. Within the profession, the fortunes of digital humanities have waxed and waned: after an early period of enthusiasm, during which the promise of this new approach was perhaps oversold, a backlash has set in. But these are early days still, and the quantitative revolution has just begun. I don't think digital humanities will do away with other methods, as some critics of digital humanities fear, but it will be a crucial new tool we can use for approaching databases and for asking questions that are larger—and smaller—than the default twenty to seventy years most studies in literary history focus on.

15. Wai Chee Dimock, *Through Other Continents: American Literature Across Deep Time* (Princeton: Princeton University Press, 2006). Also see Mads Rosendahl Thomsen, "Posthuman Scale," *CounterText* 2, no. 1, (March 15, 2016): 31–43.

16. On the side of world literature, discussions have been focused, mostly, on questions of the canon, what gets included and what doesn't, and much less on how those canons are read and used. I want to encourage a fuller engagement with modes of reading with the hope that such an engagement would open world literature canons, whatever they are, to environmental concerns (among others). I know, based on my own experience, that there will continue to be limits on how much editors can change world literature anthologies, driven as such changes must be by what teachers want to assign. While *canons* change slowly, and respond to many different requirements, *modes of reading* can change more easily, more nimbly.

CHAPTER FIVE.
STORIES FOR THE FUTURE

1. Elizabeth Kolbert, *The Sixth Extinction: An Unnatural History* (New York: Henry Holt, 2014).

2. Among the scholars using digital methods in environmental studies, I want to single out Matthew Schneider-Mayerson and his "The Influence of Climate Fiction: An Empirical Survey of Readers," *Environmental Humanities* 10, no. 2 (2018).

3. Vladimir Propp, *Morphology of the Folktale*, first edition translated by Laurence Scott with an introduction by Svatava Pirkova-Jakobson, second edition revised and edited with a preface by Louis A. Wagner (Austin: University of Texas Press, 1968).

4. Joseph Campbell, *The Hero with a Thousand Faces* (New York: Pantheon Books, 1949). The book is partially based on Sir James George Frazer, *The Golden Bough: A Study in Comparative Religion* (London: Macmillan, 1890).

5. Naomi Oreskes, *Merchants of Doubt: How a Handful of Scientists Obscured the Truth on Issues from Tobacco Smoke to Global Warming* (New York: Bloomsbury Press, 2010).

6. My understanding of settler colonialism is shaped by Mahmood Mamdani, in such works as "Settler Colonialism: Then and Now," *Critical Inquiry* 41, no. 3 (2015): 596–614, and, more recently, *Neither Settler nor Native: The Making and Unmaking of Permanent Minorities* (Cambridge: Belknap, 2020).

7. One of my favorite accounts is by Bruce Chatwin, who had a lifelong fascination with nomadism in its various forms, in *The Songlines* (New York: Viking, 1987).

8. My own, small foray into thinking about nomadism in the last few hundred years took the form of the book *The Language of Thieves: My Family's Obsession with a Secret Code the Nazis Tried to Eliminate* (New York: Norton, 2020).

9. These charts are based on research I did for my book *Poetry of the Revolution: Marx, Manifestos, and the Avant-Gardes* (Princeton: Princeton University Press, 2006).

10. Such a collective agent should not be understood as a universal figure but as a kind of differentiated collectivity, one that allows for highly targeted attributions of responsibility, harm, and blame while also acknowledging a collective destiny. For example, if almost all humans, today, are settlers or, in any case, settled, in the sense of depending on an agricultural lifestyle, this new collective agent could be thought of as an unsettled settler, settlers that have come to terms with the problems caused by settlement.

11. For a convincing argument in favor of species histories of humans, see Dipesh Chakrabarty, "The Climate of History: Four Theses," *Critical Inquiry* 35, no. 2 (Winter 2009): 197–222, 212ff.

12. See, for example, Anna Lowenhaupt Tsing, *The Mushroom at the End of the World: On the Possibility of Life in Capitalist Ruins* (Princeton: Princeton University Press, 2017).

13. My thinking about species is influenced by Donna J. Haraway's *The Companion Species Manifesto: Dogs, People, and Significant Otherness* (Chicago: Prickly Paradigm Press, 2003). Also see Mads Rosendahl Thomsen and Jacob Wamberg, "The Posthuman in the Anthropocene: A Look through the Aesthetic Field," *European Review* 25, no. 1 (2017): 150–165. For an excellent survey on posthumanism, see Mads Rosendahl Thomsen and Jacob Wamberg, *The Bloomsbury Handbook of Posthumanism* (London: Bloomsbury, 2020).

14. The *Norton Anthology* is a small episode in this history in that Norton managed to dominate the college textbook market by coming up with the right sort of paper, thin enough to allow for a maximal concentration of literature between two covers, but just thick enough to allow students to take margin notes.

15. A pressing question about storytelling in the Anthropocene is its relation to science. Many writers and critics bristle at the thought of "merely" communicating the results of climate science to a larger public, perhaps understandably so: who wants to be pressed into such a subservient position? But perhaps this

is the wrong way to think about it. A collaboration led by a former student of mine has taught me that the act of translating scientific papers can be enormously creative and important. Gloria Benedikt has developed ways of turning science papers into performances by combining dance, recorded video, and interactive games. She always involves scientists; in fact she works at a science institute as a resident artist and artistic researcher. One of her shows was performed as part of a recent United Nations summit in New York.

Turning scientific papers into stories and performances is just one of many ways in which writers and scientists can and should collaborate. Storytelling does not need to be restricted to translating science, but it should be informed by science, in the sense that it should not find itself in contradiction with the best available research on environmental change. This conviction is the core of a project, also initiated by Benedikt, call *Stories for the Future* (I am also affiliated with this initiative). Calling for stories that are informed by science does not mean that science is the only source of knowledge. On the contrary, this initiative envisions all kinds of story traditions taken from world literature to feed into this project, and it will be open to new scientific developments as well. When it comes to environmental change and literature, literature and science need to work more closely together than has hitherto been the case.

What follows is our project statement:

Stories for the Future:

After centuries of progress, the future has become uncertain again. Every morning brings news of a new plague: dead bees are dropping from the skies; the seas are suffocating; and deserts are swallowing arable lands. We don't know when, but we know that it is coming. And that's how the story ends.

But does it? And which story are we talking about?

Humans are storytelling animals. We tell stories to make sense of the world and our place in it. Stories connect us to the past, to great causes beyond ourselves, and they offer glimpses of the future. They have mobilized individuals and groups into action across the span of human history and contributed to reshaping the world.

The power of stories to shape history is part of the greatest of all stories: the evolution of life on earth. Life records and processes information through DNA, which relies on random gene mutations observed over millions of years. But the emergence of language has allowed one species, homo sapiens, to develop an additional way of recording and processing information: cultural transmission. Cultural transmission does not rely on random gene mutations, but on the deliberate transmission of knowledge encoded in stories from one generation to the next. Culturally transmitted information has been so powerful that in a few hundred thousand years—an evolutionary blink of an eye—it allowed homo sapiens to take dominion over the earth.

For hundreds of thousands of years, oral stories stored information in memorable forms, allowing specialized bards to pass them down. Then five thousand years ago, this rapid process of information storage was supercharged by the invention of writing. Proverbs and stories could be written down, preserved, and transported farther afield. New areas of knowledge emerged, from organized religion to philosophy, preserved on clay tablets and other early forms of writing. Recorded on external storage devices, this information could even survive a break in transmission and be rediscovered by future generations.

Over the last five thousand years, written stories have allowed territorial empires to expand their cultural power to distant realms. Alexander the Great was inspired by Homer to embark on his conquest of Asia and exported the Homeric epics throughout his vast empire. Portable scriptures such as the Hebrew Bible allowed Jews to retain their identity in exile. The teachings of philosophers and prophets such as Buddha, Confucius, Socrates and Jesus introduced new ideas and ways of life, ushering in an age of universal philosophies and religions. The first novels, such as those of Murasaki Shikibu, offered new ways of understanding individual identity, and science told new stories that explained the origin of life and its evolution. Manifestos, aided by the printing press, called on the literate masses to change the world through revolutions.

Today, our world is faced with new challenges, from global warming to the fourth industrial revolution, that require action on a global scale. But some of the collective stories that have steered human action in the recent past, from nineteenth-century progress to world revolution, have lost their power. As a result, we have reverted to old stories: plagues and floods ushering in the apocalypse. We are lacking new stories at the exact moment when we need them most. What kind of stories could help us through the current evolutionary bottleneck and propel us into a sustainable future? Which stories that didn't make it into the written record, or that have been marginalized, might help us now? And where can we find them?

Many of the universe's mysteries, which have been communicated through stories for most of history, have been unraveled by science. Yet scientific papers and reports are not the only—and maybe not the best—medium to help us imagine the future. We need new kinds of science-based stories, combining the two powerful tools we possess: storytelling and knowledge.

Stories for the future offers resources for writers to generate new stories that meet the sustainability challenges of our time and build an open platform to collect and publish such stories.

STORIES FOR THE FUTURE offers resources for writers to generate new stories that meet the sustainability challenges of our time and builds an open platform to collect and publish such stories.

1. Commitment to convey scientific insight

The role of the artist is slightly different from the traditional approach (i.e., Tolstoy: the role of the artist is to convince the audience of his own ideas). The challenge is to stay committed to scientific findings while employing a language that humans are naturally equipped to understand: stories.

2. Exploration of ethical dilemmas

The role of the artist is to embed scientific knowledge and insights into personal stories and highlight the ethical dilemmas that arise from those insights.

3. Dedication to embracing complexity

Many new findings in sustainability science would provide excellent material for tragedies, or dystopian science fiction novels. Or it might be tempting to create works with happy endings so that we all feel better about our collective fate. Neither is likely to help us move toward a sustainable future. A constructive approach that embraces the complexity of our situation entails a realistic assessment of where we are, a recognition of the need for grieving, and a positive vision of the path forward that can propel us into action.

4. Orientation toward action

The work does not explicitly tell audiences what to do but is designed to prompt questions: "Now that I can see the impact that scientific insights will have on my life and on our world, what can I do?"

Stories for the Future is a test to see whether we can inspire artists to undertake new forms of storytelling, an incubator for new approaches to literature. Whether it succeeds remains to be seen.

17–18; narratives and mitigation of, 8–9, 36–37, 109–110, 117–118n3; planetary consciousness and solutions to, 66; rate of, 6; settled life and destabilization of ecosystems, 26 (*See also* settled life); world literature as document of, 10–11, 26–27, 35–37, 67 (*See also specific works*)

climate justice, 9, 92–94

climate zones, Humboldt's theory: of, 62–64, *63*

coal, 5, 7

Cod: A Biography of the Fish that Changes the World (Kurlansky), 78

CO_2 levels, 2, 5, 10, 92–93

collective storytelling, 105, 106

colonialism, 9; and destruction of indigenous literature, 43, 47; and export of cultural values, 41–42, 46–47; Goethe's rejection of nationalism and, 57–59, 64, 66–67, 71; literature as complicit in, 66; Mali and French, 50; Mesoamerica and Spanish, 46–47; and religion, 46–47; "settler colonialism" and settlers as figures, 95; and universalism, 126n7; and world literature, 58, 66; and

written language, 41–42, 46–47, 50

commodity histories, 78

The Communist Manifesto (Marx and Engels), 68–70, 97–102; collective agency and the proletariat in, 97–98, 101–102; translation and circulation of, 98–100; as world literature, 98–100

The Companion Species Manifesto (Haraway), 104

comparative literature, 42, 65–66

complexity, 7–9, 61–62, 134n15

complicity of literature: in climate change, 27; in colonialism, 66; and insights into environmental change, 86; in justification of human intervention in ecosystem, 51; and justification of settled life, 41, 51, 84–85; in resource extraction, 36–37, 38, 41, 51, 53, 66–67, 70, 74, 84–86, 108; world literature and understanding the, 53

Cortés, Hernán, 2, 42–43

Covid-19, 103–104

cuneiform writing, 14, 38–39

curation, 106

Damrosch, David, 73

"deep-time" reading, 84

Denecke, Wiebke, 79

tlement in, 20–22, 24, 26; Utnapishtim and the flood story in, 16, 26; and written language, 14–15, 38–39

Epic of Sunjata: and agriculture, 49; compared to *Gilgamesh* and *Odyssey,* 49; exile from home in, 48–49; and Islamic tradition, 50; and oral tradition, 48, 50–51, 77; written versions of, 50

evolution: and adaptation to environment, 2–4; Darwin's theory of, 62–64; of humans, 3–4; and sudden climate change, 6

exile, 35, 48–49, 99

extinction events: asteroid collision, 1–2; human caused, 3, 5–7, 87

films, apocalyptic narratives in, 86

fire, 4, 7, 21, 25

floods: and climate change, 15; environmental engineering and flood control, 18, 27; Noah and Flood in the Hebrew Bible, 14–17; in *Popul Vuh,* 44; Utnapishtim's story in *Gilgamesh,* 16–17

food: agriculture and diet, 22; beer and bread in Mesopotamia, 20, 22, 25; *dado* in *Sunjata,* 49; fire and cooking,

4; maize, 43–47; omnivory and human evolution, 3

forests, 5, 23–25

fossil fuels. *See* oil

Fuchs, Barbara, 79

future, stories for the, 87, 106–107, 130–134n15

Georgics (Virgil), agriculture in, 32–33

Ghosh, Amitav, 35

Gilgamesh. See Epic of Gilgamesh

globalization: and ecology, 64–65; economic, 64, 66–70, 82, 98; environmental consequences of, 67; and environmental thinking, 59–64; Marx and Engels and economic, 68–70, 98; and planetary consciousness, 66; and translation, 58–59; and world literature, 52–53, 57–59, 66–67, 82

Goethe, Johann Wolfgang von: and environmental thinking, 59–61, 69; Humboldt as influence on, 61–66; science and search for original forms (*Urpflanze*), 59–62, 64; and world literature as concept, 53–61, 75–76

Guns, Germs, and Steel: The Fates of Human Societies (Diamond), 78

large-scale thinking: and
"deep-time" reading, 84;
world literature and, 42,
52–53, 79–80, 83–84, 86,
91, 97–98, 126nn7–8; and
"zooming in" *vs.* "zooming
out," 52, 79, 86
Layard, Henry, 14
Lebanon, 24–25, 27
Levine, Caroline, 79
Lewis, Pericles, 79
libraries, 14, 53, 75–77, 107; Anna
Amalia Library, Weimar,
75–76, *76*
literacy, 66–67, 107–108; and
persistence of orality, 48
literary criticism: ecocriticism,
9–11, 14, 51, 84–86, 87, 118n8,
119n9; and environmental
reading protocol, 84–86;
and oral tradition, 51;
structuralism and decon-
struction as method, 79;
typologies of stories and,
88–92
literary studies: and anthologies
(*See* anthologies); and
climate change, 10–11;
comparative literature,
42, 65–66; empirical, 88;
nationalism institutionally
embedded in, 71–72; quan-
titative, 83; and shaping
power of stories, 87–88;
and story typologies, 88–92.

See also literary criticism;
world literature
literature: as complicit (*See*
complicity of literature);
division of labor and production of, 4–5, 41–42;
industrialization and mass
production of, 106; orig-
inality and individual
authorship, 105–106; and
preservation of continuous
tradition, 105. *See also*
written language

Mahabharata, 70
maize, 43–47
Mali: French colonialism in, 50
Manchester, England, 69, *69*
manifestos, as genre, 101–104
Marx, Karl, 68–71, 97–102; and
collective agency, 97–98,
101–102, 105; on world literature, 67–68
Maya civilization: and agriculture, 43–46; collapse of,
45–46; preservation of
Council Books by scribes,
47–48; Spanish colonialism
and, 46–47; urbanization
and, 45; and written lan-
guage, 42–43. See also
Popul Vuh
McNeill, J.R. and William, 78
memory, 44, 51
metallurgy, 30

Mimesis (Auerbach), 78

monsters, encounters with
    non-human: Enkidu in
    Gilgamesh, 19–20, 41;
    Humbaba in *Gilgamesh,*
    23–25, 41; Polyphemus in
    Odyssey, 29–32; trickery and
    defeat of, 20, 22–23, 29–31

morality: animal fables and
    moral instruction, 33–34;
    and blame, 93–95; and
    flood as divine punishment,
    15–18; Hebrew Bible as
    influence on current, 17;
    written language and
    export of cultural values,
    41–42

Musk, Elon, 17

narratives: and agency, 92–93;
    and communal identity,
    132n15; and complexity,
    7–9; as complicit in cli-
    mate change, 27; cooper-
    ation and shared, 8; cura-
    tion and preservation of,
    107; human identity and
    "species stories," 120n20;
    as misleading, 8; and
    mitigation of climate
    change, 8–9, 36–37, 109–110,
    117–118n3; as motivation,
    8; and self-justification,
    36–37; shaping power of,
    87–88; story typologies,

88–92, *90. See also* litera-
    ture; storytelling, humans
    as storytellers

nationalism: and anthologies,
    73–74; and collective
    agency, 103–104; Goethe's
    rejection of, 57–59, 64, 66–67,
    71; and literary canons,
    71–72; Marx and Engels'
    rejection of, 67–68, 71; and
    world literature, 57–59,
    118–119n8

nature writing, 9, 27, 36–37,
    118–119n8

Naturgemälde (Humboldt),
    62, *63*

Natya-Shastra (Bharata Muni), 91

Noah and the Flood: compared
    and contrasted with
    Gilgamesh, 14–18

nomads, 22, 85, 95–96

*Norton Anthology of Western
    Literature,* 82–83

*Norton Anthology of World Lit-
    erature,* 77–83, 81

novels, environmental reading
    of, 34–36

Odyssey (Homer): agriculture
    in, 28, 31–32; city dwelling
    privileged in, 28–29, 31–32;
    compared to *Sunjata,* 49;
    Cyclopes in, 28–32, 41;
    Goethe's reading of, 60;
    hospitality in, 29–30, 32;

and line between civilization and barbarity, 31–32; metallurgy in, 30; Polyphemus in, 29–31, 41; resource extraction, trade and commerce in, 29–30, 32

oil, 5, 7, 93

Old Testament: story of Noah and the Flood in, 14–17

orality: and memory, 51; recovery of oral knowledge, 50–51; relationship of written literature to, 33, 48, 50–51, 61, 85; and *Sunjata*, 48, 50–51, 77; and world literature, 52–53

Overstory (Price), 104

Panchatantra, 33–34, 105

Poetics (Aristotle), 89

Polyphemus (*Odyssey*), 29–31, 41

population growth, 5–6, 16–18

Popul Vuh: agriculture in, 43–46; animals in, 44; creation story in, 43–47; floods in, 44; translation and preservation of, 47–48

Propp, Vladimir, 90

protagonists: and concentration of agency, 92; as heroes, 25, 91–92, 94; in Vonnegut's typology of stories, 89–90

protocol for environmental reading, 84–86

Purdy, Jedediah, 27

Ramayana, 70

Ravitsh, Melech, 70

realist fiction, 35–36

refugees, 96

resource extraction: commodity histories, 78; and forests, 5, 23, 24–25, 27; in *Gilgamesh*, 24–27, 38, 41, 66; industrialization and acceleration of, 69–70; literature as complicit in, 36–37, 38, 41, 51, 53, 66–67, 70, 74, 84–86, 108; Marx and Engels and promotion of, 70; in the *Odyssey*, 29; oil and coal, 5, 7, 93; and settled life, 4–5, 24–25, 27, 84; in Virgil's *Aeneid* and *Georgics*, 32–33. *See also* colonialism

Salt: A World History (Kurlansky), 78

scale, narrative and, 6–10, 42; world literature and large-scale thinking, 42, 52–53, 79–80, 83–84, 86, 97–98, 126nn7–8

Schelling, Friedrich, 65

scientific documents as literature, 130–134n15

settled life: and agriculture, 4–5, 20, 45–46, 86; and destabilization of ecosystems, 26; in *Gilgamesh*, 20, 24–26, 41; humans and,

circulation and access to texts, 65, 75–77; and climate change, 10–11, 27, 35–37, 67; and colonialism, 46–47, 58–59, 66–67; *The Communist Manifesto* and, 98–100; and ecocriticism, 9–11, 14, 84–86; and ecology of culture, 64–66; and environmental reading practices, 73, 74–75; and globalization, 52–53, 57–59, 66–67; Goethe's "invention" of, 67, 75–76; and large-scale thinking, 42, 52–53, 74–75, 79–80; Marx and Engels on, 67–68; and orality, 52–53; origins of concept, 53–59; and planetary consciousness, 66; and translation, 14–15, 58–59; widespread and different perceptions of, 70–71; and world consciousness, 53

written language: and acceleration of human development, 4–7; and agriculture, 32, 42, 43; alphabetic systems for, 47; and colonialism, 46–47, 50; cuneiform writing system of Mesopotamia, 14, 39–40, 132; and division of labor, 4–5, 41–42; and export of cultural values, 41–42; glyphic systems for, 47; and literacy, 66–67, 107–108; Mesoamerican invention of, 42–43; and orality, 33, 48, 50–51, 61, 85; printing technologies and, 42, 48, 51, 53, 85, 106, 108; and record keeping, 40, 66–67; and social status, 33, 42, 66–67; and territorial expansion, 39–42; as treacherous, 121n1

Yiddish language and literature, 70, 71

Zheng Zhenduo, 70–71
"zooming in" and "zooming out," 52, 79, 86